BOBBIE REED AND REX E. JOHNSON

bible
learning
activities

youth · grades 7 to 12

G/L REGAL BOOKS™

INTERNATIONAL CENTER FOR LEARNING

A Division of G/L Publications, Glendale, California, U.S.A.

© Copyright 1974 by G/L Publications. All rights reserved. Printed in U.S.A.

Second Printing, 1975

Third Printing, 1976

Published by Regal Books Division, G/L Publications, Glendale, California 91209, U.S.A.

Library of Congress Catalog Card No. 73-87520. ISBN 0-8307-0239-3

Cover photo by Gary Conniff

Text photos by David Pavol

CONTENTS

THE AUTHORS

Bobbie Reed was raised on the mission field of Brazil, and attended Arizona Bible College in Phoenix, Arizona. She has been teaching Sunday School, working with Vacation Bible Schools and Bible clubs, and co-sponsoring youth groups for sixteen years in several churches across the United States.

For the last three years Bobbie has been writing Junior High and Adult curriculum for Gospel Light Publications and contributing teaching tips to *Teach* magazine.

Recently Bobbie has been developing and conducting supervision and management training courses for the California State Department of Public Works in Sacramento, where she is employed.

Beginning life as a "missionary's kid" in the country of Bolivia, Rex E. Johnson later came to the States and finished his schooling at UCLA to obtain his Bachelor degree, then on to Talbot Theological Seminary for his Master of Religious Education.

His ministry in the southern California area has involved him in directing college/career young people and youth evangelism in Palm Springs and Catalina Island.

He is currently Minister of Christian Education in a local church and an instructor at Talbot Seminary. He has also authored *Ways to Plan and Organize Your Sunday School—Youth* published by Regal Books.

OTHER *ICL INSIGHT* BOOKS FOR YOUTH:

Ways to Help Them Learn: Grades 7 to 12, David A. Stoop
Ways to Plan and Organize Your Sunday School: Grades 7 to 12, Rex E. Johnson.

Part I

Learning Readiness

"WHAT AN OPPORTUNITY!"

"It's the chance of a lifetime!"
"Now, that's an offer you don't get every day!"

If you overheard these statements what would you suppose to be the topic under discussion? Money? Speculation? Business? Crime? Fame? Teaching a Sunday School class of young people?

While teaching a Sunday School class probably would not be the first thought brought to your mind by the above statements, they do apply to teaching.

WHAT AN OPPORTUNITY!

Teaching a Sunday School class of young people provides an opportunity for you to grow spiritually. And you will renew your joy in the Lord as you teach, for nothing is so thrilling as sharing the exciting truths of God. And because young people will always bombard teachers with hard-to-answer questions, you will be challenged and motivated to anticipate their questions and to find the answers in advance!

For these and many other reasons, through teaching, you will be kept actively involved in learning about and living by God's Word! What an opportunity!

IT'S THE CHANCE OF A LIFETIME!

Teaching a Sunday School class of young people provides a chance for you to share the benefits of your personal Christian experiences. You can share the consequences of mistakes you have made, giving reality to an otherwise theoretical discussion. The lessons you have already learned will be reinforced anew as you teach. It's the chance of a lifetime!

NOW, THAT'S AN OFFER YOU DON'T GET EVERY DAY!

Teaching a Sunday School class of young people allows you to reach young people for Christ. And it allows you to then influence the young people who will become tomorrow's Christian leaders. As a teacher you can change negative attitudes, instill spiritual knowledge and develop valuable skills for living the Christian life. Influencing the youth of today takes time and continued effort. Teaching a Sunday School class will give you the needed regular contact with a group of young people which you may not otherwise have. Now, *that's* an offer you don't get every day!

This book is the third in a series of International Center for Learning textbooks designed to help train Sunday School workers in the youth division. It is planned to help you make the most of your teaching opportunity!

The needs of the learners and lesson preparation are discussed in Part I. Part II of this book is a handbook of Bible Learning Activities which can enhance the sessions and increase the learning potential of each session.

Much of the printed curriculum you will be issued as a Sunday School teacher will include teaching suggestions for getting your learners involved in the lesson. However, you may need to look for additional ideas for reaching your own particular learners!

You may wish to teach creatively, using varied techniques and high-impact methods!

Well, here's our world of creativity—and welcome to it!

CHAPTER ONE

ARE THE LEARNERS READY?

THIS CHAPTER WILL HELP YOU TO:

1. Name six kinds of needs learners have.
2. List the three parts of a Sunday session.
3. Give three reasons for using Bible Learning Activities.

Carol absent-mindedly bumps into a chair as she enters the Sunday School classroom, knocking the chair over and very nearly knocking herself down as well! Startled out of her reverie by the loud clatter, she quickly looks around the room and breathes a heartfelt "Thank goodness!" when she sees that it is empty. She sits down in a chair and within seconds is absorbed in her problem once again.

Last night she and her boyfriend Dan quarreled and broke up!

Carol has a problem! She is miserable! Carol has a need!

In fact, each learner who comes to class has a particular basic need all his own. For example:

Jay has been looking for a part-time job all week and still has not found one. Janice is not getting along with her parents. Pete is flunking geometry and might even be kicked off the school's football team if he does not get his grades up. Pam has a terrific cold! Randy's grandmother died on Tuesday.

As each learner enters the room he is greeted by a friendly smile from Loren, the Sunday School teacher.

Just as the last learner enters the room, a bell rings; it is time for class to begin. Loren walks to the front of the room, well-prepared and ready to teach a great Bible lesson, full of meaningful and relevant truths.

But, are the learners ready to learn???

Not really. Each learner is preoccupied with his own thoughts, feelings and needs.

SINK OR SWIM

The teacher who plunges immediately into a heavy Bible lesson in order to "utilize every possible second" will not be teaching a "full house!" At best, he may have the partial attention of some of his learners! For positive results, Christian educators today advocate an alternative approach to teaching.

A BETTER WAY

Years of research and evaluation of commonly used teaching techniques have resulted in some new approaches to helping young people learn the Bible. These approaches could be summarized this way: *Identify and use the learners' needs as a technique of helping them learn.*

WHAT NEEDS?

Educators classify all of man's needs into five basic groups. They are: physical, security, social, self-respect and achievement. Christian educators add one more group: spiritual needs. These needs could be visualized as an ascending stairway which learners must climb in order to learn.

A learner's spiritual needs cannot be met until his other basic needs have been quieted. In other words, a Christian teacher must set the stage for learning by identifying and using the needs of his learners to help them learn the great truths of God's Word. For example,

LEARNING

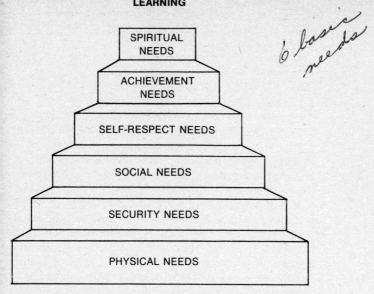

6 basic needs

if a learner needs to achieve, help him *do* something successfully!

LET'S TAKE IT ONE STEP AT A TIME!

1. *LEARNERS HAVE PHYSICAL NEEDS FOR:* warmth, comfort, mobility and all other physical necessities. For example, a learner who comes to Sunday School hungry will find it hard to concentrate on learning.

And, because a hot, stuffy room almost always prevents learning, a teacher needs to maintain a comfortable room temperature, plan a good seating arrangement, check the lighting, and plan activities which allow students to move around.

In other words, a wise teacher will recognize these physical needs and by meeting them, will provide a conducive environment for learning.

2. *LEARNERS HAVE SECURITY NEEDS FOR:* belonging to a group, abiding by a few recognized rules, being allowed to disagree, and not being afraid to say something stupid, of being put down, or of having to be one hundred percent perfect all the time.

A teacher can meet some of these needs by allowing learners to work in teams to formulate joint effort answers. He can set up classroom rules stating that everyone's opinion may be honestly expressed and respectfully disagreed with. A teacher can make it easy to say, "I could be wrong! You might be right!"

In other words, a wise teacher recognizes these security needs and provides a non-threatening environment so the young people can learn.

3. *LEARNERS HAVE SOCIAL NEEDS FOR:* fellowship, conversation, work groups, helping each other, loving and being loved, accepting others and being accepted, sharing the feelings of others and having others share their feelings.

A teacher can get to know and befriend each of his learners individually. A teacher can plan for and build group spirit within the class. A teacher can help class members accept each other by discouraging criticism of each other. And whenever possible a teacher should encourage learners to relate personal experiences which illustrate the lesson truths, creating a give-and-take group relationship.

In other words, a wise teacher recognizes the social needs of his learners and provides an atmosphere of warm fellowship in order to meet these needs.

4. *LEARNERS HAVE SELF-RESPECT NEEDS FOR:* knowing and understanding the facts, receiving and giving attention, respect, courtesy, acceptance, understanding and praise.

A teacher can plan activities in which learners do research, brainstorm and discuss ideas, solve problems and report to the other learners on various joint or individual projects.

An important function of the teacher is to reassure each learner who volunteers an answer in class of the value of his contribution. Comments should be prompt and positive.

A wise teacher recognizes the self-respect needs of his pupils and meets those needs by providing, drawing out and affirming each learner in class.

5. *LEARNERS HAVE ACHIEVEMENT NEEDS FOR:* using their abilities, discovering and trying out ideas and

growing as a person. The perceptive teacher can organize classroom learning experiences into a course for a learner in the most beneficial way. In a way, a teacher is really a guide to his learners because learning and achieving takes place within the learners' own experiences.

A wise teacher recognizes the achievement needs of his learners and meets those needs by helping his class members set and reach realistic and meaningful learning goals.

6. *LEARNERS HAVE SPIRITUAL NEEDS FOR:* hearing the Word of God (Romans 10:17); the gift of grace (Ephesians 2:8,9); experiencing the changes which accompany the new life in Christ (2 Corinthians 5:17); learning concern for others rather than for self alone (Philippians 2:3,4); knowing that Christ has the answer for everyone (Philippians 4:19); experiencing the fulness and guidance of the Holy Spirit (John 16:13); becoming familiar with and believing in and practicing the Word of God (2 Timothy 3:16,17); overcoming temptation (1 Corinthians 10:13); sharing what they learn (Galatians 6:6); being encouraged to continue in the Christian life even on ":down days" (Galatians 6:7-9); understanding spiritual truths (2 Timothy 2:7); praying (John 16:23,24); fellowship with other believers (1 John 1:7); identifying with Bible characters as human beings similar to themselves in many ways (1 Corinthians 10:11,12); transformed lives that prove God's will (Romans 12:1,2).

A teacher can pray for the Holy Spirit's help during the week while preparing the lesson so that each learner will receive individual personal understanding through the lesson. Scriptural truths presented in the lesson can be reinforced with discussion, debate, Bible research or other learning experiences. A wise teacher recognizes the spiritual needs of his learners, and plans for positive changes in their lives by meeting these needs.

DON'T FORGET!

A teacher needs to remember that the learners' spiritual needs cannot be met until their other basic needs are not paramount. Unless the learners feel they are achieving something in Sunday School, any spiritual learning could be said to be incidental and seldom of lasting value. This presents Sunday School teachers with a problem to consider.

WHAT'S MY JOB?

A Sunday School teacher's primary function is to meet the spiritual needs of his learners. He plans his unit objectives and lesson with each learner in mind so that through personalized goals he can further the spiritual growth of each class member. Is he also expected to minister to the basic needs of his learners? Why, there isn't enough time in Sunday School! Or, is there. . . ?

Yes, there is time.

One way to meet many needs in the allotted time is to use Bible Learning Activities. Bible Learning Activities are planned experiences which help learners understand and explore scriptural truths. These experiences include individual and group assignments, and they range from discussion to dramatic and musical activities.

Each phase of the Sunday School session has a special purpose. The *Approach* captures the learners' interest; the *Bible Exploration* involves learners with God's Word; and the *Conclusion* and *Decision* helps the learners personalize and apply the biblical truth they explore.

THE APPROACH

Those first few vital minutes of a session make up the *Approach* phase. The *Approach* serves two main purposes:

1. Meeting the learners' basic needs, and
2. Familiarizing the learners with the lesson content.

Let us look at the first purpose: "meeting the learners' basic needs." Go back and read the first few paragraphs of this chapter, and think about each learner's basic needs. Jot down what you would do to meet the basic needs of the young people described.

Now, consider some different Bible Learning Activities which could provide opportunities for developing group spirit, for being accepted, for sharing, for using capabilities, for being recognized, for fellowship, etc. *Any Bible Learning Activity which involves the learners in working together can help meet the basic needs of each learner.*

"Involves" is a key word. The *Approach* activity acts as a magnet, drawing together and focusing the thoughts, interest and concentration of each learner on the lesson topic.

"Together" is another very important term. Group interest is desired, so the teacher needs to build group feeling and spirit during the first few minutes of a session, rather than focusing on the individual achievement or opinions of the learners. *Approach* activities normally do not include debates, long reports, or problem-solving assignments; these would not best meet the learners' needs. This does not prevent having the learners meet in small groups at the beginning of the session. However, if this is done, there should still be a "togetherness" atmosphere within each small group, created by a perceptive teacher with "together" Bible Learning Activities.

Another reason for avoiding detailed discussion during the first few minutes of a session is explained by the second purpose of the *Approach* phase of the session.

Let us look at that second purpose: "familiarizing the learners with the session topic." The selection of *Approach* Bible Learning Activities is simplified when a teacher remembers that during the first few minutes of a session he wants to introduce the lesson content.

Learners are very conscious that they are living in the "now". In order to meet them where they are with his *Approach* activity, the teacher needs to use activities which relate to the present.

THE BIBLE EXPLORATION

The *Bible Exploration* segment of the session follows the *Approach* activity. The *Bible Exploration's* one main purpose is to meet the learners' spiritual needs by grounding each learner in God's Word with positive and practical application.

Imagine that you are Loren, the Sunday School teacher mentioned at the beginning of this chapter. You have planned to develop a session on Prayer with your class. What spiritual needs related to the session topic might you have listed for learners before class? Spiritual needs are very real; yet, when these young people came to class they probably did not feel these spiritual needs!

Many young people coming to Sunday School do not actually *feel* any spiritual need; they are apt to be more conscious of their other basic needs than of their spiritual needs. But, a teacher needs to remember that the Holy Spirit knew ahead of time who was going to attend the class and what lesson would be needed. And if the teacher asked the Holy Spirit's guidance in planning the session, then the lesson is exactly right.

SPIRITUAL ASPIRINS AND PREVENTIVE MEDICINE

Ministering to the needs of learners is a two-fold process:
1. After class, the teacher deals individually with the learner who feels a spiritual need unrelated to the lesson.
2. The teacher plans his lessons so that over a given period of time (for example, a quarter), he has covered the main areas of all of his learners' spiritual needs.

The teacher succeeds in his ministry by systematically teaching God's principles and truths from the Bible and then helping the learners to apply these principles to any of their specific problems and needs. This is a practical method. It works! If Christian young people are ever to have "the mind of Christ" they must be consistently and continually taught from and grounded in God's Word.

A teacher who has well-rounded, long-range teaching plans provides his learners with a well-balanced spiritual diet. A young person bouncing from one crisis to another comes to Sunday School looking and hoping for spiritual aspirins which should be administered individually. But the young person who lives victoriously in spite of crises, is one who has benefitted from a weekly dose of spiritual preventive medicine—a diet of sound, practical Bible lessons. During a *Bible Exploration* the Holy Spirit sometimes persuades individual learners to apply the spiritual truth of the lesson to a need in their own lives. Or, sometimes a Scripture passage suddenly comes alive to one of the learners through the illumination of the Holy Spirit. In these ways, the teacher and the Holy Spirit become partners in helping the learners through a well-planned Bible session.

A Bible session that is well-designed and prepared is one that uses one or more appropriate Bible Learning Activities which directly involve the learners in researching, discussing, analyzing and understanding the lesson Scriptures and truths during the *Bible Exploration* part of the session.

THE CONCLUSION AND DECISION

The final phase of the session is a time of *Conclusion and Decisions.* (Sometimes the printed curriculum subdivides this phase into two segments: lesson conclusions, and decisions for living.) This phase has one purpose: "encouraging learners to apply the lesson truth to the 'today' circumstances of their daily lives."

The Bible learning of the session is summarized and reinforced during the *Conclusion and Decision* activities.

ISN'T TELLING THE TRUTH ENOUGH???

Christian educators are sometimes asked why Bible Learning Activities are needed. If a teacher has pinpointed his learners' spiritual needs and if he has found scriptural solutions for those needs—is not just telling the scriptural truth to the learner enough?

No! In the book, *Ways to Help Them Learn, Youth,* David Stoop explains that learning is a process *accomplished by the learner.* Bible Learning Activities help the learners digest the spiritual diet provided them by the teacher, because the learners are given a chance to *become involved* with God's truths. Learners discover spiritual truths for themselves, explore God's Word, try God's principles, and practice living the Christian life through Bible Learning Activities!!! Telling passes on information, but involvement leads to real and lasting learning.

BUT HOW DID JESUS TEACH???

Jesus was a great teacher and leader. As God, He was well aware of the individual spiritual needs of each of His disciples and of those whom He met every day. But Jesus did not just take each person aside and tell him what he should know or ought to do! Instead, Jesus carefully chose His words and His teaching techniques to meet the spiritual needs of His learners. Luke records some of the interesting learning activities Jesus used. They are listed below:

Reference	Learning Activity
Luke 2:41-52	Listening and asking questions
Luke 4:16-21	Scripture reading
Luke 5:5-11	Demonstration
Luke 5:34,35	Illustration
Luke 6:9-11	Rhetorical question
Luke 6:20-38	Discourse
Luke 7:36-50	Contrast
Luke 8:4-15	Parable and explanation
Luke 9:1-10	Projects
Luke 10:29-37	Analogy
Luke 11:1-4	Model
Luke 13:6-9	Parable
Luke 13:18-21	Comparison
Luke 18:15-17	Rebuke
Luke 18:18-30	Dialogue
Luke 20:1-8	A form of Agree/Disagree
Luke 20:21-26	Audio-visual aids
Luke 21:1-4	More audio-visual aids
Luke 22:55-62	A well-timed glance
Luke 24:44-53	Illumination

Young people have basic and spiritual needs which can be met in a well-planned Sunday School session. The Bible lesson needs to be planned to answer the learners' needs. The Bible Learning Activities need to be carefully chosen in order to bring the need and the solution together in a learning experience for each learner.

Planning a successful Bible lesson and choosing the best Bible Learning Activities for the session are discussed in the next chapter.

INSTANT REPLAY

1. Name six kinds of needs learners have.
2. List and describe the main function of the three phases of a Sunday School session.
3. Give three reasons for using Bible Learning Activities in teaching.

ONE STEP BEYOND!

1. Skim the Gospel of Mark (there are only sixteen short chapters!) and list the different learning activities Mark records that Jesus used.

2. Think back to the last Sunday School class you taught (or attended). List the Bible Learning Activities which were used. How did those activities help the learners get involved in the lesson topic and scriptural truths?

3. Finish this sentence expressing your personal opinion:

"I believe that Bible Learning Activities . . ."

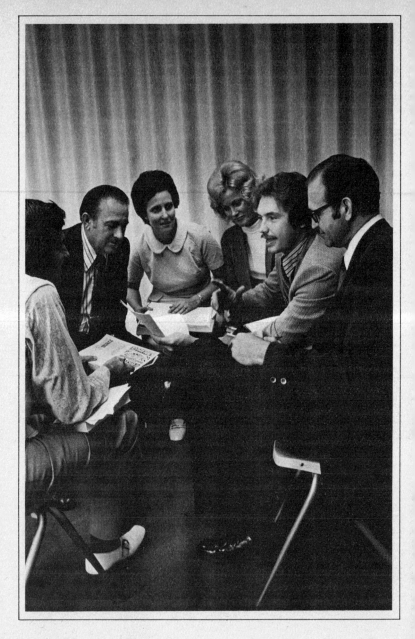

CHAPTER TWO

IS THE TEACHER READY?

THIS CHAPTER WILL HELP YOU TO:

1. Define a unit of study and list the steps in Unit Planning.
2. Explain the relationship between a session and a unit, and arrange the steps of Session Planning in order.
3. State which of the above steps should be done by individual teachers before a Departmental Planning meeting.

"I thought you only hired experienced computer programmers, Bill! Now, if that's true, then why did you schedule those eight new programmers for thirteen solid weeks of classroom training before putting them on a project? The way I look at it, that's just lost production time, Bill, and I don't see how I can approve this training budget of yours!"

Bill, the training coordinator for the computer systems department, nodded his understanding of the company accountant's confusion. "I know how it must look on paper, Cliff, but let's take a tour of the department and I think you'll get a clearer idea of the situation."

The two men walked through the company's computer center. A few minutes later in the cafeteria, over a cup of coffee, Bill explained.

"Our training schedule is designed to reduce such costly job failures. You see, even a highly skilled computer programmer must be oriented to our company's computer system. All companies are not alike; they all have different program needs. And you have to deal with each need on an individual basis—just as you do with people!

"In a large company as computerized as ours is, Cliff, those thirteen weeks of initial training are absolutely essential for a new programmer. Without that preparation he would be totally ineffective on the job!"

WHAT PRICE EFFECTIVENESS???

In a Sunday School teacher's planning meeting that night, Cliff shared with the other teachers.

"My company won't trust a programmer even to touch paperwork without extensive preparation. Yet, I'm ashamed to confess that sometimes I've dared to walk into a Sunday School classroom, hoping to make some changes in my learners' lives, and virtually ad-libbed a lesson because I had failed to prepare the way I should have!

"What I need to remember, what we all need to remember, is that all learners are not alike and that it takes a lot of preparation on our part *before* the sessions. We need to adapt the curriculum to our individual learners' needs and to consider what changes in their lives God would have us plan for!"

Cliff has a very good point! Adequate preparation is the price of effective teaching.

THE FIRST STEP

Scheduling a regular time early in the week for planning is the first step to successful preparation.

PLAN THE UNIT

A unit of study is a series of 2-5 sessions covering the same general topic. Each session of the unit spotlights one facet of the topic. Most curriculum is written in units of two or more lessons per topic. When scheduling the unit, the teacher will have to check how many Bible lessons there are in the unit and assign each lesson to a specific session.

WRITE THE UNIT THEME

The unit theme defined in the printed curriculum is intended to be more than just a convenient title. The theme is the unifying idea for the lessons and as such should be kept in mind throughout the entire unit.

UNIT OVERVIEW

Unit dates: _March 3, 10, 17, 24_

1. Unit theme: _How it begins_

STATE THE CENTRAL TRUTH TO BE TAUGHT BY THE UNIT

Sometimes Bible lessons are grouped very closely into units of study, and sometimes it seems that they are grouped very loosely.

Perhaps the best method of finding the central truth of the unit is for a teacher to *read the unit Scriptures* and draw his own conclusions. A teacher can write a short sentence stating the main point of each chapter or passage and then summarize those main points into one central truth. (The individual chapter or passage summaries can be used when planning the individual lessons to tie each lesson into the unit.)

---

2. Unit Central Truth:
   a. The Bible passages for this unit: ① _Matthew 6:5-15;_ ② _John 1:1-5,_ ③ _Colossians 1:15-17;_ ④ _Romans 5:6-8;_ ⑤ _John 16:5-15_

   b. The Central truth of each passage and lesson: _____
      1. _God knows your needs so pray to him._
      2. _Jesus is, and has always been, God, the creator._
      3. _All things were created through Jesus and for him._
      4.&5. _Christ died for us & sent the Holy Spirit to guide us._
   c. So, the Central truth of the unit is: _Jesus, through whom a creation was accomplished, died for us. Now through the Holy Spirit God who knows our needs, wants to help and guide us._

After writing out the main points of each passage, a teacher may select one of the passages as a key to the others. For example:

For example: the central truth of the unit above was actually a summary of all of the central truths of the 4 sessions:

1) Christ died for us and sent the Holy Spirit to guide us

. . . which shows that:

2) God knows our needs so we can depend on and pray to Him

. . . praying helps, because:

3) Jesus is, and has always been, God, the creator

. . . meaning that:

4) All things were created through Jesus and for Him

. . . so therefore the central truth of the unit would be:

Jesus, through whom creation was accomplished, died for us. Now, through the Holy Spirit, God, who knows our needs, wants to help and guide us.

LIST THE SPIRITUAL NEEDS OF THE LEARNERS TO BE MET BY THE UNIT

A teacher needs to constantly remember that his job is teaching people—not just communicating curriculum content! He takes into account that each class member has his own set of personal, spiritual needs. When planning a unit, a teacher lists each of his learners by name and then tries to identify the specific, spiritual need of each learner with relation to the unit's central truth. Ideally, a teacher will have no more than eight to ten learners so he can effectively minister to each.

3. The needs of the youth in my class to which the unit passages may speak:

NAME	NEED
Greg	A real relationship with Christ - maybe salvation
Scott	Practical experience in sharing his faith
Lee	To let God guide him
Rick	To express trust in Christ
Dave	Daily reliance on God, even in tough times
Steve	To yield his cares to the Holy Spirit
Bob	Boldness through the power of the risen Christ

4. If they apply the central truth of this unit to their individual needs, by the end of this unit, my class members should be able to:
   a. Describe how their relationship with God affected a life decision they made
   b. Plan how they will rely on God for guidance and care
   c. Experience sharing Christ with a friend
   d.

SET UNIT GOALS

The unit goals are a general statement of the result of each learner's applying the central truth of the unit to his own spiritual need. Some teachers help learners achieve unit goals by sharing the goal with the class at the beginning of the unit. Therefore, unit goals must be specific and easily understood by the learners. And then specific goals are set for each learner based on the general unit goals. Specific goals are those which define or imply *a change in the learner's behavior.* True learning takes place only when a person's actions change after being introduced to a new idea, concept or belief.

   Unit goals may be more complicated than session goals. But a more complicated goal is realistic for a unit because there are several sessions in which to work towards accomplishing that goal. The Sunday School teacher can help his learners make the desired changes in their lives by prayerfully setting unit goals.

UNIT OVERVIEW

Unit dates: _____

1. Unit theme: _____
2. Unit Central Truth:
   a. The Bible passages for this unit: _____
   _____
   _____
   b. The Central truth of each passage and lesson: _____
   _____
   _____
   _____
   _____
   c. So, the Central truth of the unit is: _____
   _____
   _____
   _____

For example: the central truth of the unit above was actually a summary of all of the central truths of the 4 sessions:
_____

. . . which shows that:
_____
_____
_____
_____

. . . praying helps, because:
_____
_____
_____
_____

. . . meaning that:
_____
_____
_____

. . . so therefore the central truth of the unit would be:
_____
_____
_____
_____

3. The needs of the youth in my class to which the unit passages may speak:

NAME	NEED
_____	_____
_____	_____
_____	_____
_____	_____
_____	_____
_____	_____
_____	_____
_____	_____
_____	_____

4. If they apply the central truth of this unit to their individual needs, by the end of this unit, my class members should be able to:
   a. _____ _____
   b. _____ _____
   c. _____ _____
   d. _____ _____
   e. _____ _____

TIE EACH SESSION INTO THE UNIT

When the teacher has completed the four steps just described, he will have an excellent one-page overview of the unit which is a handy and helpful reference when planning the individual sessions. A unit is like a two-, three-, or four-step job; and each session is like one step of the job! Each step must be carefully planned or the job may fail!

PLAN THE SESSIONS

A good foundation of unit preparation is virtually useless if the session construction is haphazard and careless. The seven steps in planning a good session are:
1. Review the unit overview.
2. Write down the central truth of the Scripture passage(s).
3. List the spiritual needs of the learners to be met by the session.
4. Set session goals.
5. Select Bible Learning Activities.
6. Write out Teaching Plan.
7. List ways to involve specific learners.

REVIEW THE UNIT OVERVIEW

Each session is planned individually, but each must be carefully coordinated with the others in the unit.

First, the teacher notes and writes down the date, number, central truth, theme and general goal of each session.

This step is designed to help the teacher remain unit conscious, which will measurably increase his teaching effectiveness.

WRITE DOWN THE CENTRAL TRUTH OF THE SESSION

Nothing could be more devastating to a Sunday School session than a vague idea of what is to be taught. Writing down a specific central truth from Scripture helps a teacher be specific in his teaching.

LIST THE SPIRITUAL NEEDS OF THE LEARNERS TO BE MET BY THIS SESSION

When listing the spiritual needs of the learners to be met by the session, the teacher reviews the list he made when preparing the unit. He then selects and copies only those needs which are linked to the central truth of the lesson at hand. The lesson should be carefully planned to meet those specific needs of one or more of the learners. A unit will meet some of the spiritual needs of all the class members; a session may also be generally helpful to all but primarily tailored to meet the specific needs of just one or two of the learners.

SESSION OVERVIEW

1. Review the Unit Overview:
   a. Session Number: _1_   Session Date: _3-3-74_
   b. Unit theme: _How it begins_
   c. The Central truth of the unit: _Jesus, through whom creation was accomplished, died for us. Now, through the Holy Spirit, God, who knows our needs, wants to help and guide us._
   d. The general unit goal: _for their relationship with God to affect the lives of the learners in a positive way that they can describe_
2. The central truth of the session passage is: _God knows your needs, so pray to him._
3. The needs of the youth in my class to which the session passages may speak:

NAME	NEED
Lee	To let God guide him
Rick	To express trust in Christ
Dave	Daily reliance on God even in tough times
Steve	To yield his cares to the Holy Spirit

SET SESSION GOALS

When setting session goals, a teacher starts with adapted lesson aims in the curriculum.

A statement of session goals always starts with *"By the end of this session my learners should be able to":* This wording forces a teacher to be learner-centered in his goals. That is, the goals are written in terms of what the learners should be able to do rather than what the teacher should be able to do.

If learners leave Sunday School with the knowledge and/or feeling that they have reached one or more goals they will usually consider their time well spent.

Further help in writing goals is given in Chapter 7 of *Ways to Help Them Learn; Youth*, by David Stoop, and Chapter 7 of *Ways to Help Them Learn; Adults*, by H. Norman Wright.

---

4. By the end of the session, the above learners should be able to:
find specific Bible verses which give God's promises to Believers and describes how each promise should apply to decisions, situations and problems they face each day.

SELECT BIBLE LEARNING ACTIVITIES

Keeping in mind the session goals, the learners' needs, and the lesson's central truth, a teacher considers several Bible Learning Activities which are appropriate for the session. He then chooses the best activities from the list.

Even though printed curriculum usually suggests several possible activities, the teacher needs to always consider MANY different Bible Learning Activities in order to select the most effective ones for the session.

---

5. Some possible Bible learning activities for meeting the goals, the learner needs and presenting the central truth of the lesson:
Neighbor-nudging - "What is God like?"
Crayon drawing a "Your Concept of God"
Buzz groups a "How is God like your father? How not?"
Paraphrase - Rewrite verses into "God, I promise to..."
Letterwriting - Thank God for those promises you plan to use this week
Lecture - "God's promises are to Believers - are you one?"

WRITE OUT TEACHING PLAN

Some of the Bible Learning Activities selected may be suitable for large groups and may be planned for the departmental time of the session when all the classes in the department meet together. If so, each activity requires a teacher to supervise it.

Some of the Bible Learning Activities chosen will be best suited for small groups. These should be scheduled when each class or small group studies individually.

Some Bible Learning Activities chosen will be best suited for individual exploration. These also need to be thought through and planned carefully.

Next, the Bible Learning Activities are organized into a workable schedule, or teaching plan. The time allowed, the materials needed, and the specific responsibilities for each activity should be included.

This teaching plan goes into class with the teacher to help him conduct an effective session.

LIST WAYS TO INVOLVE SPECIFIC LEARNERS

The last step in session preparation is planning how to get individual learners involved in the learning experiences.

A teacher who takes these seven steps will walk into class well prepared and capable of effecting positive changes in the lives of his students.

---

6. Teaching Plan

TIME SCHEDULE	BIBLE LEARNING ACTIVITIES CHOSEN (indicate D or C)	SUPPLIES NEEDED	SPECIFIC RESPONSIBILITY
9:30 - 9:45	1. Crayon drawing "Your Concept of God" (D)	Drawing paper crayons	Dept. Superintendent
9:45 - 9:55	2. Buzz groups "How is God like your father? How not?" (C)	—	Teachers
9:55 - 10:10	3. Paraphrase - "Rewrite versus "God, I promise to..." (C)	list of verses Bibles pencils paper	Teachers
10:10 - 10:25	4. Letter writing "Thank God for His promises" (C)	paper, pencils, envelopes	Teachers
10:25 - 10:30	5. Lecture - "God's promises are to Believers - are you one?" (D)	chalkboard, chalk, Bible	Dept. Superintendent

7. I plan to involve individual learners in the session by: _____

Lee - Ask to share his ideas first for activity 2

Rick - Ask to share his ideas to help others get started on activity 3

Dave - Distribute supplies for activity 04

Steve - Write on chalkboard for activity 5

TEAM PLANNING

The preparation techniques described in this chapter are also practical in a Sunday School where team teaching is used and planning is a shared responsibility. Before the team planning meetings, each teacher works through all four steps of unit planning (steps one through three of session, and the activity selection part of step four), for themselves and bring their notes to the meeting.

All the individual ideas are shared and discussed. Changes are made and new ideas are conceived. Through cooperative group effort, a teaching plan develops that will be truly workable—and better than any one individual teacher's plan!

HINDSIGHT IS 20-20

Good teachers are always learning how to improve their techniques by taking a few minutes after a session for an honest self-evaluation. They make notes about what should have been done differently and what worked well. These notes are dated and kept for use in future sessions.

INSTANT REPLAY

1. Define a unit of study.
2. List and briefly describe four steps of unit planning.
3. Explain the relationship between a session and the unit.
4. Arrange in order the seven steps of session planning listed below:
   Set session goals.
   List ways to involve specific learners.
   Select Bible Learning Activities.
   List the spiritual needs of the learners to be met by the session.
   Review the unit overview.
   Write out teaching plan.
   Write out the central truth of the session.
5. State which of the above steps are done by an individual teacher before a departmental planning meeting, and explain why.

ONE STEP BEYOND!

1. State the central truth of the unit described below:
Theme: How We Got Our Bible
Lesson 1—2 Timothy 3:14-17
Lesson 2—2 Timothy 3:14-17; 2 Peter 1:21
Lesson 3—Nehemiah 8:1-8; Acts 8:26-39
Lesson 4—Matthew 28:16-20

2. List three of your learners (or three young people you know well) and write a spiritual need of each which relates to the central truth of the above unit.

3. Write specific unit goals for all three learners. In other words, how will their lives be changed if they apply the central truth of the unit to their own spiritual need?

Part II

Handbook of Bible
Learning Activities

"An idea is not a suggestion until you write it down!"
read a company poster advocating employee suggestions! Part II of this book is a handbook of suggested
Bible Learning Activities. Each began with an idea, but
each has been tried and proven successful all across
the United States by Christian teachers and leaders in
churches of all sizes.

In any given situation there are probably several Bible
Learning Activities which would be effective. New and
different activities add the element of surprise to the
sessions. Therefore, a growing teacher resists the temptation to fall back on a few familiar activities and to
neglect the unfamiliar ones. In a constant search for
ways to improve his teaching effectiveness, every
teacher should try *each* Bible Learning Activity suggested in this handbook, at least once! He owes it to
learners and to himself!

SELECTION CODES

Choosing which Bible Learning Activities to use has
been simplified by the use of selection codes after the
name of each activity in this handbook. Each Bible
Learning Activity is coded in three ways to help a teacher
in selecting the activities to use in the session.

1. The letters A, B and C indicate in what part of the
session the activity is to be used: in the *Approach, Bible
Exploration* or *Conclusion* phase of the session. Some
activities may work well in more than one phase of the
session.

2. The numerals 7,8,9,10,11 and 12 will indicate the grade level with which this activity is most effective. Some activities are better suited to junior high learners than to senior high young people. But a creative teacher can adapt almost any activity to suit any age level!

3. The letters S and L will indicate appropriateness of the learning activity for small groups or large groups. In some cases both S and L will appear indicating that the activity works well with both small groups or large groups.

When both large groups and small groups are used at different times during the activity, the recommended teaching procedure will be shown as follows:

L-S— Large group, then small groups
S-L— Small groups, then large group
S-L-S— Small groups, then large group, then small groups again
L-S-L— Large group, then small groups, then large group again. For more information on what is meant by large groups and small groups, read chapter three in the book *Ways to Plan and Organize your Sunday School* by Rex Johnson.

A FEW HINTS

As vital as learner participation is, it is only a tool to help the learners reach the unit and session goals.

Instructions for a chosen Bible Learning Activity should be clear, complete and as concise as possible. Learners should be told what to do, what the purpose of the activity is and how long they have for the activity. If the instructions are in the least complicated, they should probably be written out and copies duplicated for the learners.

AND REMEMBER

If you're a teacher, you've been entrusted with influencing the spiritual progress of your learners. God's truth is waiting to be taught, so go ahead . . .

CHAPTER THREE

TELL IT!

Lecture techniques are those in which the communication is essentially one way, i.e., from speaker to learners.

USE LECTURE BIBLE LEARNING ACTIVITIES TO:

Relay a quantity or "block of information" in a relatively short period of time.

Lecture techniques do have their place in a Sunday School session. They are most efficient for the entire department as one large group, making announcements or giving instructions or information which concern the entire group.

Whenever possible, lectures should be accompanied by illustrative audio-visuals to maintain the learners' interest and make the learning more lasting. The effectiveness of different teaching techniques is diagrammed on the next page:

Each of the following lecture techniques is designed to make telling God's truths effective and interesting.

CHORAL READING (C;10-12;L-S-L)*

Help the learners build a script that personalizes the Bible truths which have been explored. Then divide the class into two groups and give copies of the script for

*See Introduction Part II for explanation of codes.

A LECTURE BIBLE LEARNING ACTIVITY

PHYSICAL	SECURITY	SOCIAL	SELF-RESPECT	ACHIEVEMENT	SPIRITUAL
	–do not require learners to do anything but listen –inform and explain	–can entertain			–expose learners to God's Word and truths –present an entire concept without interruption –expose learners to outside talent and knowledge (eg. films, speakers, etc.)

a choral reading. Each group decides which parts of the script to read, and you read the rest. Much of the learning takes place while learners are preparing for the presentation by carefully studying the Scriptures, writing the script, discussing and deciding which words and phrases should be accentuated. Reassemble the class and allow the members to present the entire script.

DISCOVERING CHORAL READINGS

Many of the Psalms were written for and used by the Israelites as choral readings; they can be used in today's Sunday School classes as lecture activity simply by reading them.

Another way of using a choral reading is to prepare a paragraph response to each line or sentence of a psalm. Then one or more of the class members reads each of the psalm lines, and the rest of the class members respond with their paragraphs—singly or in unison. Here is an example from Psalm 8:

Teacher: "O LORD, our Lord, How majestic is Thy name in all the earth,"

Class in unison: "God, your name is spoken in every language with awe and reverence. Even men who deny your existence respond to the intricacy of your handiwork."

EXPLORING CHORAL READING POSSIBILITIES

Based on the session aims and the specific needs of the learners, choral readings can help learners to:
1. Share the Israelite poetry.
2. Read the lesson Scriptures.
3. Respond to the lesson Scriptures.

CHECKLIST OF MATERIALS NEEDED

Script for the reading

DEMONSTRATION (A,B,C;7-12;L)

The teacher shows the students how something was done historically, how something should be done, or how to operate a piece of equipment.

DISCOVERING DEMONSTRATIONS

To make Judges 6,7 come alive, a teacher might demonstrate how Gideon threshed his grain. He would need to buy a small sack of wheat from which the chaff had not yet been removed. If this were not available, he could buy some peanuts and shell them, leaving the dark brown "chaff" mixed in with the peanuts. Then, spreading a sheet on a table, the teacher would toss the grain or peanuts into the air, straight up, eight to ten inches. Then, placing an electric fan about eighteen inches from the pile and tossing the grain or peanuts again the teacher could show how important the wind was to Gideon's threshing efforts.

Demonstration of Bible customs, clothing, culture and architecture need to be a part of any lesson where these have a bearing on the truths to be learned.

Demonstrating behaviors which should result from Bible teaching will give your learners a model for changing their lives. As Bible study or conclusion activity, a teacher might demonstrate ways to share Christ with a friend, or possible ways to worship God.

EXPLORING DEMONSTRATION POSSIBILITIES

Based on the session goals and the specific needs of the learners, demonstration can help the learners to:
1. Understand a strange custom or activity.
2. Visualize spiritual concepts.
3. Discover desirable behavioral changes.

CHECKLIST OF MATERIALS NEEDED

_____ Chalkboard, a large flipchart or blank overhead transparency with an appropriate writing instrument (and a projector if the transparency is used)

_____ Large pictures, posters, illustrative graphs or maps

_____ Any other necessary props or equipment

FILM (B,C;7-12;L)

Filmed Bible stories, missionary experiences and "today" pictures of cities and countries mentioned in the Bible are often available to a teacher from a local supplier.

DISCOVERING FILMS

Films and filmstrips can be misused easily; careful planning for their proper use is indicated. Although many Christian films are entertaining, that is not why they were produced. They each have a message.

Another common misuse of films is to use them as "fillers" on national holiday Sundays when several teachers are going to be gone. If a film does not develop a unit of study, it should not be used!

A film can become a discussion or drama activity if the learners are asked to respond to it in some way (see Chapters 4 and 6).

EXPLORING FILM POSSIBILITIES

Based on the session goals, and the specific needs of the learners, films can be planned to:
1. Illustrate the lesson truth.
2. Expose learners to Bible customs or lands.
3. Share missionary experiences.

CHECKLIST OF MATERIALS NEEDED

_____ Sound film, slides or filmstrip
_____ Projection screen
_____ Projector

INTERVIEW (B;7-12;L)

There are several types of interviews, most of which will be discussed in Chapter 4. But as a lecture activity there is a special function for an interview.

DISCOVERING INTERVIEWS

When a guest speaker or a teacher cannot conduct a long monologue, an interview can be used to make the speaker's format a series of answers.

To use the technique, ask the speaker to prepare a list of questions for a class member to ask him as a way of delivering the lecture material he plans to present.

For example, if the topic were "Science and the Bible," a questioner could voice the questions nonbelievers often raise and then the speaker would answer each question as it is asked.

This technique can be used to help an inexperienced speaker. The question and answer "interview" can even be practiced before class if necessary. Other types of interviews are suggested in Chapter 4.

EXPLORING INTERVIEW POSSIBILITIES

Based on the session goals, and the specific needs of the learners, interviews can help learners to:
1. Appropriate truths presented by a speaker.
2. Listen to and learn from a long lecture by a speaker.
3. Learn to present effective lectures.

CHECKLIST OF MATERIALS NEEDED

_____ Well-planned notes on the subject to be covered
_____ Well-phrased questions

MONOLOGUE (B;7-12;L)

Jesus' Sermon on the Mount recorded in Matthew 5—7 is a sublime example of a monologue. Although monologue, most often known as "the lecture method," is often overused and misused, it can be very powerful. Who has never been moved by an eloquent speaker?

DISCOVERING MONOLOGUES

One effective use of monologue is to paint a picture using words. The objective is to help the learners visualize the setting and the action of a Bible story.

Another use of monologue is as a summary of what has been accomplished during a session or a unit. Sometimes a series of Bible Learning Activities moves so quickly through a one-hour session that a short review is necessary for your learners to see the importance and inter-relationships of the various learning activities. In this case, your monologue should last no longer than three minutes and include:

1. A statement of the session objective.
2. A quick review of the results of each Bible Learning Activity.
3. A two to three sentence description of life changes that are called for by the Scripture passage studied.
4. And a call for decision and commitment.

Obviously this kind of monologue needs to be well planned for its impact will be lost if it becomes general and repetitive.

EXPLORING MONOLOGUE POSSIBILITIES

Based on the session goals, and the specific needs of the learners, monologues can be planned to:
1. Paint a word picture.
2. Summarize the session or unit.
3. Review the main truths in the session Scripture.
4. Challenge the learners to make decisions and commitments.
5. Reinforce the continuity of a unit.

CHECKLIST OF MATERIALS NEEDED

_____ Well-planned notes on the subject to be covered
_____ Chalkboard, a large flipchart or a blank overhead transparency with an appropriate writing instrument (and a projector if the transparency is used)
_____ Large pictures, posters, illustrative graphs or maps

RECORDED STORY (B,C;7-12;L)

Tape-record a Bible story, a personal testimony, or a missionary story before class time and play it at the appropriate time in the session. Carefully select the material to be recorded. The recording needs to be clear and easy to hear and understand so the learners will benefit from the experience.

DISCOVERING RECORDED STORIES

A "recorded story," is especially suited for use as research material that is unavailable at the time of the report such as "pastor's comments," interview material, or special effects which will add to a Bible story.

Set up the recording and player before class. Adjust the volume so that everyone can hear.

EXPLORING RECORDED STORY POSSIBILITIES

Based on the session goals, and the specific needs of the learners, recorded stories can be used to:
1. Enhance a presentation.
2. Present information from outside sources.
3. Introduce a unit of study.

CHECKLIST OF MATERIALS NEEDED

_____ Recording
_____ Player for the recording

SYMPOSIUM (B;11,12;L)

Three or more well-prepared speakers present their opinions on an issue. The speakers sit in front of the entire department facing the learners. A symposium differs from a panel; symposium speakers do not discuss their opinions; they simply present ideas.

If a question and answer session has been scheduled to follow the symposium the learners may ask the speakers questions about what has been said during the presentation.

DISCOVERING SYMPOSIUMS

Job's "friends" were an interesting symposium—each had an opinion about why Job was suffering!

A symposium needs to be well-controlled by the department superintendent or a teacher, a fact that should be understood ahead of time by the symposium members. Otherwise one of the members might proclaim his views to the exclusion of the other members' views.

EXPLORING SYMPOSIUM POSSIBILITIES

Based on the session aims and the specific needs of the learners, symposiums can be designed to:
1. Present various viewpoints on a topic.
2. Explore an issue.
3. Introduce controversial subjects or ideas.

CHECKLIST OF MATERIALS NEEDED

_____ Table
_____ Three or more chairs in front of the classroom facing the learners
_____ Large name cards for the speakers

LECTURE TECHNIQUES ARE SUCCESSFUL WHEN TEACHERS:

1. Assemble needed materials before class.
2. Set up room before class.
3. Use lecture techniques sparingly.
4. Keep lectures short and interesting.
5. Use audio-visuals as often as possible.
6. Have students take notes and list questions they have.
7. Show enthusiasm.
8. Make sure everyone can hear speakers, film, or recording.
9. Combine lecture techniques with discussion and/ or other participation activities whenever possible.

AND WHEN TEACHERS:

1. Do not expect students to sit still and listen to a long boring presentation.
2. Do not expect students to remember everything that is presented.

YOUR NOTES: (Complete the following sentence.)

When I used lecture techniques . . .

CHAPTER 4

DISCUSS IT!

Discussion is a deliberate two-way conversation between two or more people on an assigned topic.

USE DISCUSSION BIBLE LEARNING ACTIVITIES TO:

Explore an issue from several different viewpoints.
Expose learners to information and resources which
will help them solve their personal problems.
Give the teacher an indication of where the learners
are in the learning process.

Discussion teaching techniques quickly involve the learners in the lesson by focusing their interest and attention on one topic or question.

Starting a discussion and keeping it going is easy if a teacher follows one basic rule: *Ask a question which cannot be answered with "yes" or "no".*

Most discussion techniques can be used best in small groups. The purpose for using the technique in the session determines whether discussion will take place in small or large groups. If the discussion technique is to prepare for the main lesson activity and is used merely to stimulate thinking, then use large group discussion. If learner participation is the purpose for the discussion technique, then small group discussion is used to get as many learners involved as possible.

A helpful teacher plans his sessions around various discussion techniques in order to meet both the basic

A DISCUSSION BIBLE LEARNING ACTIVITY

PHYSICAL	SECURITY	SOCIAL	SELF-RESPECT	ACHIEVEMENT	SPIRITUAL
—relieves tension, helps learners relax —changes the interest center easily	—develops a healthy mental attitude —is a learning experience —builds group spirit —organizes ideas	—provides for sharing of self —develops friendships —is a give-and-take conversation —can be done in groups of two or more —encourages learners to help each other learn	—promotes understanding and acceptance of self and others —gives opportunity to be courteous and respectful of others	—provides for fulfilling one's potential —allows using one's capabilities —exposes students to new ideas	—summarizes learning —underlines truths in learners' minds —crystalizes spiritual principles —links the spiritual to the practical —provides Christian fellowship —allows teacher to check understanding of the learners

and spiritual needs of his learners as shown in the following chart.

Each of the following suggestions for discussion techniques can be used without any visual aids or hand-out material. The discussions will be more profitable, however, if some of the suggested materials in the checklist are provided with each technique.

AGREE-DISAGREE (A,C;9-12;L or S)*

Agree-Disagree statements differ from true-false in that usually there may be no "right" answers to the statements or questions.

DISCOVERING AGREE-DISAGREE

Make up a list of debatable statements (about five to ten) about the lesson topic and give each learner a duplicate copy of the statements.

Each learner marks an "A" beside those with which he agrees, and a "D" beside those statements with which he disagrees. Discussion of the statements can take place either in a large group or a small group.

An agree-disagree discussion is a good way to introduce the lesson topic and to get the learners involved in expressing their own opinions on the subject. Definite answers to the statements need not be decided upon; the activity is basically designed to generate discussion and interest, not to settle issues.

EXPLORING AGREE-DISAGREE POSSIBILITIES

Based on the session goals and the specific needs of the learners, agree-disagree can be used to:
1. Introduce the session topic.
2. Involve the learners with the session truths.
3. Generate lively discussions.
4. Initiate research in order to discover answers to the statements.

*See Introduction Part II for explanation of codes.

CHECKLIST OF MATERIALS NEEDED

_____ Copies of five to ten debatable statements
_____ Pencils
_____ Clear instructions

BRAINSTORMING (A,C;7-12;L or S)

Write a question on the chalkboard, a large flipchart or an overhead transparency. The students quickly suggest several answers. No evaluation is made when suggestions are given.

DISCOVERING BRAINSTORMING

Brainstorming is an excellent interest-catching activity which stimulates thinking about an idea which is to be developed later in the session. Ideas usually come quicker under the pressure of a deadline, so five minutes is a good maximum time limit for brainstorming.

EXPLORING BRAINSTORMING POSSIBILITIES

Based on the session aims and the specific needs of the learners, brainstorming may be planned to:
1. Introduce the session topic.
2. Draw out many opinions or ideas quickly.
3. Involve learners with the lesson topic.
4. Discover several possible answers to a question.

CHECKLIST OF MATERIALS NEEDED

_____ Chalkboard
_____ Chalk
_____ A statement or question for learners to respond to

And sometimes . . .

_____ Lined paper
_____ Pencils

BUZZ GROUPS (B,C;7-12;S)

A class of up to eight learners, or small groups of three to five learners each from a class are called buzz groups.

DISCOVERING BUZZ GROUPS

When the learners reach a point in the lesson development that they need to consider the facts presented this far and need to come to a conclusion or decision before proceeding, divide the large group into small classes, or the class into buzz groups of three to five learners each and appoint a leader in each group. In these groups the learners briefly share ideas with each other and come to a decision which is later shared with the other class members or the department by the group leaders.

Provide written instructions if the buzz-group assignment is to compare several Scriptures or consider more than one question.

EXPLORING BUZZ GROUP POSSIBILITIES

Based on the session aims and the specific needs of the learners, buzz groups of learners might:
1. Discuss and report on a topic or part of the session Scripture.
2. Discuss and share their answers to one or more questions.
3. Summarize the lesson and discuss its practical applications.

CHECKLIST OF MATERIALS NEEDED

_____ Chalkboard
_____ Chalk
_____ Clear instructions
and sometimes . . .
_____ Lined paper
_____ Pencils
_____ Duplicated copies of the assignment

CIRCLE RESPONSE (A,B,C;7-10;S)

Circle response helps every learner to participate by asking him to respond in turn to a given question or statement.

DISCOVERING CIRCLE RESPONSE

Write a statement or question on the chalkboard, flip-chart or transparency and ask *each* learner in the class to respond in turn to the statement or question.

This technique works best if the chairs are in a circular arrangement. If they are not, work around the class systematically, making sure that each learner has a chance to respond. No one may speak twice until everyone has spoken once.

EXPLORING CIRCLE RESPONSE POSSIBILITIES

Based on the lesson aims, and the specific needs of the learners, circle response can be designed to:
1. Introduce or explore the lesson topic.
2. Involve the learners by sharing their personal ideas.

CHECKLIST OF MATERIALS NEEDED

_____ Chalkboard
_____ Chalk
_____ Prepared statements for learners to respond to
_____ Clear instructions

DEBATE (B,C;11-12;L-S)

A debate is a structured discussion which follows an established format and set of rules.

DISCOVERING DEBATES

At least a week ahead of time assign four to six learners to prepare for a debate presentation. Give the assignment in writing. Two or three learners prepare to argue the "for" side of the assigned issue and two or three learners prepare to argue the "against" side. Include helpful hints, suggested arguments or pertinent Scripture references in the assignment, if the learners seem to need help.

On the day of the debate, the debaters sit facing the rest of the group and present their arguments. The debate either can be informal or follow actual debating rules, with timed speeches, a timekeeper and rebuttals.

After the debate, the learners organize into small groups to discuss the truths presented by the debaters.

EXPLORING DEBATE POSSIBILITIES

Based on the session aims, and the specific needs of the learners, debates may be assigned to:
1. Familiarize learners with the session topic.
2. Present the two sides of the issue as represented by two opposing biblical characters in the session Scripture.

CHECKLIST OF MATERIALS NEEDED

_____ Duplicated copies of the assignment, with a few helpful hints
_____ Pencils
_____ Clear instructions

FILM TALKBACK (C;7-12;S)

When the main Bible Learning Activity for a session is a film, the activity should be a film "talkback" in which the learners respond to the message of the film.

DISCOVERING FILM TALKBACK

Before viewing a film, filmstrip or slide show, give the learners a copy of a list of questions to be answered and discussed after the film.

EXPLORING FILM TALKBACK POSSIBILITIES

Based on the session aims and the specific needs of the learners, film talkback may:
1. Question the information presented in the film.
2. Test learners to see how much information they absorbed.
3. Stimulate learners to relate to the truths presented.

CHECKLIST OF MATERIALS NEEDED

_____ Duplicated copies of questions for learners
_____ Pencils
_____ Clear instructions
and of course,
_____ Film
_____ Projector
_____ Projection screen

IN-BASKET (C;10-12;L-S)

Teacher gives written instructions to students during roleplay to control the course of the roleplay.

DISCOVERING IN-BASKET

Write up your regular directions for roleplay and then write further instructions for one or more of the participants. These extra instructions are given *during* the roleplay. Participants should know they may receive new instructions while roleplaying. These new instructions supersede all previous instructions.

For roleplay on Romans 12 to show the need for everyone in the body, you might originally give one participant instructions to act like a clique member during a planning session. During the roleplay give him additional instructions such as: a) suggest plans that only include kids who have been coming for a while, b) be very negative about any outreach ideas, c) emphasize that what your group needs is fellowship.

EXPLORING IN-BASKET POSSIBILITIES

In-Basket can help your learners to:
1. Raise issues they might not otherwise deal with.
2. Cope in their own way with specific attitudes in an emotionally "safe" environment.
3. See themselves with some of the pretense gone.

CHECKLIST OF MATERIALS NEEDED

___ Roleplay instructions for each participant.
___ In-Basket instructions for one or more participants.

INTERVIEW (B,C;7-12;S)

Write the assignment on the chalkboard and direct learners to work in their classes or in diads (groups of two) interviewing one another, to find out the specific information assigned by the teacher.

DISCOVERING INTERVIEWS

Learners may be interviewed as "themselves" or as an imaginary or biblical character they are role-playing.

Depending upon the assignment, a large group discussion may or may not follow the interviews.

EXPLORING INTERVIEW POSSIBILITIES

Based on the session aims and the specific needs of the learners, interviews may:
1. Draw out information quickly.
2. Allow all learners to participate in a very short amount of time.

CHECKLIST OF MATERIALS NEEDED

___ Chalkboard
___ Chalk
___ Lined paper
___ Pencils
___ Clear instructions

LISTENING TEAM (B,C;7-12;L)

When a presentation is planned for a large group, give three or four learners a special listening assignment.

DISCOVERING LISTENING TEAMS

Learners assigned to listening teams listen for implications in a Scripture passage, recording, song, missionary speaker's message, film, filmstrip, etc. After the recording or reading, each member of the listening team shares the implications he discovered, then the discussion is opened to the whole group.

EXPLORING LISTENING TEAM POSSIBILITIES

Based on the session goals, and the specific needs of the learners, listening teams can help learners to:
1. Listen more attentively to a presentation.
2. Share their impressions and ideas.

CHECKLIST OF MATERIALS NEEDED

___ Copies of the assignment
___ Pencils
___ Clear instructions

NEIGHBOR-NUDGING (A,C;9-12;L-S)

Neighbor-nudging is a special kind of discussion as opposed to couple buzzers, pairs, or diads! Two learners share with each other or work together on an assignment for one minute only, whereas diads can last as long as a teacher wishes.

DISCOVERING NEIGHBOR-NUDGING

Give the group an assignment (written or oral). Each learner turns to one of his "neighbors" and the two work on the assignment, such as a definition, an opinion, or a suggestion for one minute.

EXPLORING NEIGHBOR-NUDGING

Based on the session aims and the specific needs of the learners, neighbor-nudging is used to:
1. Develop the session topic.
2. Explore the session Scripture.
3. Share personal opinions or projects.
4. Summarize what has just been studied.

CHECKLIST OF MATERIALS NEEDED

____ Chalkboard
____ Chalk
____ Clear instructions
and sometimes . . .
____ Duplicated copies of assignment
____ Paper
____ Pencils

PANEL (B,C;9-12;L-S)

A panel is a report presentation given to the class by three to four learners.

DISCOVERING PANELS

A week ahead of time assign three or four class members to be a panel. During the week, they research the Scriptures about an assigned topic.

On the day of the panel discussion, the panel members sit facing the other learners who take turns asking questions of the panel. The questions may be directed at one specific panel member or asked of the whole panel. When there are no more questions, or after a specified time limit, the learners gather into small groups and discuss the ideas presented by the panel.

EXPLORING PANEL POSSIBILITIES

Based on the session goals, and the specific needs of the learners, panels can be planned to:
1. Expose learners to several viewpoints.
2. Develop the session topic.
3. Initiate a general discussion on a controversial topic.

CHECKLIST OF MATERIALS NEEDED

_____ Copies of the assignment for panel members
_____ Clear instructions

PROBLEM SOLVING (B,C;7-12;S-L)

Learners work in small groups to solve an assigned problem, usually involving relationships with God or with others.

DISCOVERING PROBLEM SOLVING

Thoughtfully plan the problem assignment so that the learners will readily identify with the situation. The solution to the problem should not be too obvious.

Emphasize finding scriptural answers to the problem. Appoint a leader in each group to share the group's answer when all the learners are regrouped.

A typical problem might be: ''What are some possible answers you might give to an angry father who wrongly accuses you of breaking a tool.

EXPLORING PROBLEM-SOLVING POSSIBILITIES

Based on the session aims and specific needs of the learners, problem-solving activities can be designed to:
1. Introduce, explore or apply the session truths.
2. Check whether or not the learners are assimilating the session truths.

CHECKLIST OF MATERIALS NEEDED

_____ Copies of the assignment
_____ Pencils
_____ Bibles
_____ Clear instructions

QUESTION-ANSWER (B;7-9;L or S)

The teacher guides the learners through the session truths or Scriptures with skillful questioning.

DISCOVERING QUESTION-ANSWER

Read each question aloud to the learners and have them write out then volunteer to orally give the answers. As an alternative, distribute duplicated copies of the questions, organize the learners into small groups and allow them to work together writing out the answers to the questions.

Encourage the learners to find and share biblical answers to assigned questions.

Searching the Scriptures for answers in class is great practice for turning to God's Word for answers to life's daily problems.

EXPLORING QUESTION-ANSWER POSSIBILITIES

Based on the session aims, and the specific needs of the learners, question-answer can help learners to:

1. Discover the facts of the session passage.
2. Explore the implications of the lesson truths.
3. Learn to find answers in God's Word.
4. Discover similarities between Bible texts.

CHECKLIST OF MATERIALS NEEDED

_____ Clear questions on session topic or Scripture (copies for learners are optional)
_____ Pencils

DISCUSSION ACTIVITIES ARE SUCCESSFUL WHEN TEACHERS DO:

1. Assemble needed materials before class, bringing enough for a few extra learners who may be present.
2. Set up room before class.
3. Allow free expressing of ideas.
4. Allow learners to think through their responses and write them down before calling on them to answer.
5. Set ground rules for expressing negative opinions about others.
6. Encourage 100 percent learner participation.
7. Listen carefully to what *is not* said, as well as to what *is* said.

AND WHEN TEACHERS DO NOT:

1. Look for and reinforce only ideas which coincide with your own opinions.
2. Dominate the discussion, or allow any one student to dominate the discussion.
3. Try to start a discussion by merely saying, "Take five minutes to discuss the third chapter of John."
4. Get nervous when there is silence for a few seconds.
5. Try to answer all of the questions posed by the learners—instead, turn them back to the group.
6. Let wrong conclusions go unquestioned.
7. Pretend to agree when you do not.

YOUR NOTES: (Complete the following sentence.)

When I used discussion techniques . . .

CHAPTER FIVE

WRITE IT!

Pencil and paper activities are primarily those in which learners write their ideas. The possible variations of these activities are almost infinite!

USE BIBLE LEARNING ACTIVITIES WHICH INVOLVE WRITING TO:

Clarify feelings, thoughts and ideas;
Stimulate thinking;
Allow for individual expression.

Illusive half-thoughts are often clarified and developed into full-fledged ideas when captured on paper. A written idea can be shared, analyzed, and evaluated much easier than an unwritten thought can.

Pencil and paper activities harness and channel the vivid imagination of young people. The moment a learner begins to imagine what-might-have-happened, or what-could-happen-if, his eyes begin to sparkle; he is suddenly deeply interested and involved in the lesson.

As with all Bible Learning Activities, the real value of pencil and paper activities is controlled by the teacher. His choice of appropriate activities to suit the session and his learners, his attitude about the assignment and his personal enthusiasm during the session will determine, to a large degree, the success of the activities. Pencil and paper activities can be invaluable to the teacher who sincerely desires to meet his learners' spiritual needs, but realizes that he must also meet each of their basic needs. The following chart outlines some of the benefits of using writing activities.

Take these skeleton ideas and clothe them to attract and teach your own particular learners.

DISCUSSIONS

A group discussion should usually follow a writing activity. Decide whether small or large group discussions will be the most profitable.

Most of the following suggestions may be adapted to become *either* individual or small group assignments, depending on whether you have planned to follow the writing activity with small group or large group discussion.

CHARACTER COMPARISON (B,C;7-12;L or S)*

People in the Bible can be compared or contrasted with one another or with contemporary people through the character comparison. While comparing personalities, attitudes or activities, learners identify with, respond to and learn from biblical characters.

Comparisons may be in list, chart or paragraph form.

DISCOVERING CHARACTER COMPARISONS

Learners need to know the specific purpose of writing a character comparison during the session in order to benefit from the activity. They should know what they are looking for (personality traits, attitudes, actions) and why.

If the lesson centers on the importance of a personal commitment to Christ, ask the learners to compare the commitment of two people. If a biblical character is compared to a contemporary Christian leader, supply a brief biographical sketch of the latter.

After an in-depth Bible study of a biblical personality,

*See Introduction Part II for explanation of codes.

A WRITING BIBLE LEARNING ACTIVITY

PHYSICAL	SECURITY	SOCIAL	SELF-RESPECT	ACHIEVEMENT	SPIRITUAL
—provides a physical activity during the session —provides for a familiar and comfortable learning position (if tables are used)	—develops a healthy mental attitude —provides a reachable goal for learners —provides a group experience —allows use of talents and skills —helps sort out, organize, and evaluate ideas	—allows fun and fellowship which make learning fun —builds friendships as learners get to know each other through sharing their ideas —allows meaningful and profitable conversation and discussion of ideas after writing —lets learners help each other grow —allows learners to work alone within the session and thus personalizes the learning experience	—develops a good feeling about personal ideas when they have been written and approved of by others —provides for receiving and giving recognition, attention, respect, courtesy, appreciation, acceptance, understanding, and praise —encourages understanding one's self better	—allows use of learners' potential —provides an outlet for imagination —uses capabilities —provides challenging opportunities and experiences —exposes learners to new knowledge and ideas	—helps learners define their spiritual beliefs and convictions —helps learners practice expressing their beliefs so they can later share verbally with others when witnessing —develops a "spiritual thinking gear" —allows for insight and illumination —helps teacher and learners see amount of progress in acquiring knowledge —provides avenues for evaluation of learners' understanding —allows learners to learn God's truths by discovery (especially when paraphrasing or rewriting a story from the Bible) —undergirds learners' faith as beliefs are clarified —allows for honest questioning and doubt which when expressed can be answered and eliminated —helps learners identify with Bible characters —helps the Bible come alive —helps God's truths become pratical and applicable to today's problems —provides an opportunity for learning to be individual, personal and unique with each learner

learners may become sensitive to areas of spiritual need in their own lives if, as a *Conclusion and Decision* activity, they write a character comparison of themselves and the lesson personality.

In most cases, character comparisons need to be shared and discussed with the other learners.

EXPLORING CHARACTER COMPARISON POSSIBILITIES

Based on the lesson goals, and specific needs of the learners, character comparisons might be written to:

1. Discover the similarities between two biblical characters.
2. Discover the differences between two biblical characters such as Peter and Paul.
3. Identify similarities between a modern-day missionary and a biblical character such as Barnabas or Paul.
4. Relate one's personal spiritual experiences to those of a biblical character studied in the lesson.

CHECKLIST OF MATERIALS NEEDED

_____ Lined paper
_____ Pencils
_____ Clear instructions (oral or written)

LETTER WRITING (A,B,C;7-12;L or S)

Learners write letters during a session to express personal feelings or to describe a personal experience. Assignments include letters actually to be mailed to someone, letters which might have been written by a biblical character to one of his acquaintances, and letters which might be written by people in a given situation.

DISCOVERING LETTER WRITING

Letter writing assignments are so versatile, they may be used in any phase of the session!

Most letters written by the learners need to be shared and discussed for maximum learning benefit.

EXPLORING LETTER WRITING POSSIBILITIES

Based on the session goals and the specific needs of the learners, letter writing can be assigned to:

1. Explore the possible feelings and ideas of biblical characters.
2. Outline plans to implement session truths.
3. Share personal ideas and experiences.
4. Share the session truths with a friend.

CHECKLIST OF MATERIALS NEEDED

____ Lined paper
____ Pencils
____ Clear instructions
and sometimes . . .
____ Envelopes
____ Stamps

LOG, JOURNAL, DIARY (B,C;7-10;L or S)

Writing a page from the imaginary log, journal or diary of a Bible character captures the interest of young people. This type of identification with the lesson character tends to personalize and enhance the learning process.

DISCOVERING LOGS, JOURNALS AND DIARIES

Instruct the learners to read and discuss the biblical account of a dramatic event in preparation for the writing assignment. Remind the learners that a person often expresses his innermost thoughts in a diary—the questions he would not dare ask, the doubts, the private boasting or the secret wishes.

Writing a diary, journal, or log can be a continuing project over a period of several sessions within the same unit of study. If the learners write several pages from the diary of the main character of the unit, they get an overview of and feel for the sequence of events in the life of that person.

This type of assignment is more fun and beneficial when learners share and discuss what they have written with each other.

EXPLORING LOG, JOURNAL AND DIARY POSSIBILITIES

Based on the session goals and the specific needs of the learners, log, journal and diary assignments can be designed to:

1. Compare the attitudes of two opposing characters in a story.
2. Explore the feeling of true repentance such as those David had when rebuked by the prophet Nathan (2 Sam. 12; Psa. 51).
3. Help learners sympathize with a character in order to learn from that person's experiences.

CHECKLIST OF MATERIALS NEEDED

_____ Lined paper
_____ Pencils
_____ Clear instructions

NEWSPAPER STORY (B;7-12;L or S)

Learners write a newspaper account of a biblical event, as it might have been reported in a local newspaper at the time of the event.

DISCOVERING NEWSPAPER STORIES

After they study and discuss the biblical incident of the lesson (the feeding of the five thousand or the healing of the ten lepers, etc.), learners may elect to be either believing or nonbelieving reporters.

This activity can be expanded into writing an entire newspaper representing the historical events of a unit of study. Plan to complete one or two segments of the newspaper during each session of the unit, allowing for several types of writing assignments. The paper might include: news stories, editorials, a poetry corner, a sports section, advertisements and even want ads!

Share and discuss each news story or segment of the newspaper as it is completed.

EXPLORING NEWSPAPER STORY POSSIBILITIES

Based on the session goals and the specific needs of the learners, newspaper writing provides a way to:

1. Analyze and organize the facts of a Bible story in the order of their significance and importance.
2. Tie a unit together with a continuing project.
3. Present the results of a small group study of a Bible passage.
4. Share ideas and talents with the other learners.
5. Describe an event recorded in the lesson Scripture.
6. Use creativity as a learning experience.

CHECKLIST OF MATERIALS NEEDED

_____ Lined paper
_____ Pencils
_____ Clear instructions
and possibly (for grades 10-12) . . .
_____ Typewriter
_____ Large sheet of newsprint
_____ Rubber cement

PARABLE (C;10-12;L or S)

A parable is a short, simple story which teaches an important truth. Jesus often used parables to help His listeners understand the heavenly truths He was trying to share with them.

DISCOVERING PARABLES

After learners have become familiar with a passage, ask them to write a parable based on the truth of the passage. They need to remember that modern parables need to be about familiar things and situations: parables can involve freeways, schools, games, or even refrigerators!

Parables are most valuable as *Conclusion and Decision* activities, because they provide that needed bridge between the Bible lesson and the practicalities of life. Real learning takes place when learners apply to their own lives in such a way that they are changed, what they have discovered in class.

Whether the actual writing of the parables is done by the learners as individuals, or in small groups, the learning activity is enhanced when the parables are shared and discussed.

EXPLORING PARABLE POSSIBILITIES

Based on the session goals, and specific needs of the learners, parables can be planned to:
1. Change the setting of a Bible story into a contemporary setting.
2. Paraphrase one of Jesus' parables into a modern situation.
3. Clarify spiritual truths.
4. Discover the practical aspects of the session Scriptures.
5. Summarize the *Bible Exploration*.

CHECKLIST OF MATERIALS NEEDED

_____ Lined paper
_____ Pencils
_____ Clear instructions

PARAPHRASE (A,B,C;7-12;L or S)

Learners read Bible passage and rephrase it into their own words, so that it becomes a very personalized prayer or psalm or passage.

DISCOVERING PARAPHRASES

At the beginning of a session ask the learners to paraphrase a verse or two of Scripture to stimulate their thinking along toward the lesson's main point.

A longer paraphrase assignment is more appropriate during the *Bible Exploration* phase of the lesson when learners have more time to evaluate Scriptures and decide on the meaning of a longer passage. The plan of salvation might be assigned, based on several Scripture references such as Romans 3:23, Romans 5:8, John 1:12, John 3:16, and Romans 10:13.

One learner paraphrased these verses this way:

"I have sinned and do not measure up to God's standards. But, God showed His great love for me while I was still a sinner, by sending Christ to die for me. And if I receive Him, God will give the power to become His child. All I have to do is trust God and believe in Christ.

When I believe, I will live forever, because whoever calls out to God will be saved!"

Paraphrasing is an easy but powerful Bible learning activity! The learners' paraphrases are best shared and discussed for maximum benefit.

EXPLORING PARAPHRASE POSSIBILITIES

Based on the session goals, and specific needs of the learners, paraphrases can help learners:
1. Understand spiritual truths.
2. Personalize Scripture.
3. Summarize a session or unit truth.
4. Introduce the session topic.
5. Discover the full meaning of a passage.
6. Identify with a session character.

CHECKLIST OF MATERIALS NEEDED

____ Lined paper
____ Pencils
____ Clear instructions

PICTURE SKETCH (A,B;7-12;L or S)

Display a large picture so that everyone can easily see it. Learners study the picture for a few minutes, then write about it. The writing assignment varies depending on the aim of the activity.

DISCOVERING PICTURE SKETCHES

The picture used for this activity can be a landscape, an action scene, a scene from a Bible story, or a Christian abstract drawing.

Assign the learners to describe the people, or things in the picture, or the setting of the picture. Or, ask the learners to describe what the picture says to them.

If the picture is a scene from a Bible story, ask the learners to describe the picture and then check the Scripture passage for the accuracy of the scene.

EXPLORING PICTURE SKETCH POSSIBILITIES

Based on the session goals, and the specific needs of the learners picture sketches might be used to:

1. Visualize Bible settings, or scenes.
2. Respond to an artist's idea of a scene.
3. Draw out ideas and talents of learners.
4. Get learners involved in researching Scriptures by having them verify the artist's painting.

CHECKLIST OF MATERIALS NEEDED

_____ Lined paper
_____ Pencils
_____ Picture large enough to be seen easily by all learners
_____ Clear instructions

POETRY (C;7-12;S)

Briefly explain one kind of poetry to the learners. Then ask them to write a similar poem about the events of the Bible story just covered in the lesson, or about a selected topic, about their own hopes and dreams, or about God's love.

DISCOVERING POETRY

Expose the learners to several types of poetry and allow them to choose which kind of poetry to write.

Poetry assignments often work best as small group assignments rather than as individual projects. Even people who do not feel poetically inclined can really enjoy completing and discussing a poetry assignment when working with two or three others.

Each small group of learners shares their poetry with the other groups and discusses the different meanings brought out by the various poems.

EXPLORING POETRY POSSIBILITIES

Based on the session goals, and the specific needs of the learners, poetry can be designed to:
1. Express the significance of the session Scripture.
2. Share personal experiences or opinions.
3. Summarize a session or unit truth.
4. Personalize the session truths.

CHECKLIST OF MATERIALS NEEDED
_____ Lined paper
_____ Pencils
_____ Samples of one or more different kinds of poetry
_____ Clear instructions

WRITE A PRAYER (A,B,C;7-12;L or S)

Learners write a prayer which might have been offered by a Bible character in a particular circumstance recorded in the Bible. Or, learners compose a prayer they themselves might keep and use in a recurring situation in their own lives. For example, they can write a prayer they can remember to repeat when they feel themselves getting very angry at someone.

DISCOVERING PRAYER WRITING

This is an especially good session-closing or unit-closing activity for individual learners. Prayer writing helps a person think about what he will say to God and actually involves each learner rather than just one person who might lead in an audible prayer.

Prayers written by the learners during the session can either be shared or kept private.

Two kinds of written prayers are a "litany," and a "collect."

A litany is a prayer or poem which is read responsively by two groups of people, or by a leader and a group of people. The litany is written to voice the thoughts of a group of biblical characters or to voice the petitions of the class.

Many of the Psalms and many passages in Proverbs were written in litany form.

A collect is a one-line prayer and a beautiful way to help each learner zero in on specific changes he wants to make as a result of a class session.

Example: "Father, help me use more variety in my teaching. Amen."

Jesus prayed a collect on the cross, "Father, into thy hands I commit my spirit."

EXPLORING PRAYER WRITING POSSIBILITIES

Based on the session goals and the specific needs of the learners, prayer writing can be planned to:

1. Close the session or unit.
2. Focus on specific learner needs.
3. Make a commitment to God.
4. Express personal feelings to God.
5. Share the feelings and needs of others.
6. Gain insight into the lesson characters.
7. Apply the lesson truths to learners' lives.

CHECKLIST OF MATERIALS NEEDED

____ Lined paper, or a 3"x5" card
____ Pencils
____ Clear instructions

QUESTION BOX (A,B,C;7-12;L or S)

Learners write questions to be answered by other learners or the teacher. Questions are written on small strips of paper, which are folded up and placed in a box for response.

DISCOVERING QUESTION BOXES

As a Bible study activity, learners read a Bible passage and then make up questions for each other. Learners then take turns drawing a question out of the box and trying to answer it. Questions are discussed as each is answered.

Sometimes a permanent question box in the classroom is helpful to students. Empty the question box each week and either answer the questions yourself or answer them through a group discussion.

EXPLORING QUESTION BOX POSSIBILITIES

Based on the session goals and the specific needs of the learners, question boxes can help learners:

1. Understand the meanings and implications of the session studies.
2. Discover answers to their personal doubts, or questions.

3. Identify the important facts of the session, as they write questions for fellow learners.
4. Review a session or unit.

CHECKLIST OF MATERIALS NEEDED

____ Lined paper
____ Pencils
____ Scissors
____ A medium-sized box, such as a shoe box
____ Clear instructions

SELF-EVALUATIONS (C;7-12;L or S)

At the end of a session which clearly directs the learners to present themselves wholeheartedly to God, give the learners a few minutes for self-evaluation. A self-evaluation activity need not be complicated or long.

DISCOVERING SELF-EVALUATIONS

Distribute 3"x5" cards to your learners and tell them to be very honest as they finish a sentence such as one of these:

"If I were to take this lesson seriously, I would have to . . ."

"I am like (the Bible character in the session) in that I too failed the Lord when I . . ."

"I really need to ask God's help to make a few changes in my life such as . . ."

This is an excellent activity for the last session in a unit. Evaluations may sometimes be shared and discussed, but often are more beneficial when kept confidential.

EXPLORING SELF-EVALUATION POSSIBILITIES

Based on the session goals and the specific needs of the learners, self-evaluation activities can:

1. Relate the session truths to the lives of the learners.
2. Help learners identify areas of need in their lives.
3. Encourage learners to take the session seriously.

CHECKLIST OF MATERIALS NEEDED

_____ A 3″ × 5″ card for each learner
_____ Pencils
_____ Clear instructions

STORY WRITING (A,B,C;7-12;L or S)

Story writing fits into any phase of the session, with any age group as either an individual or small group activity!

DISCOVERING STORY WRITING

Learners read a Bible story and then create a story about what happened the next day in the lives of the characters in the story. Learners learn to predict the consequences of decisions or actions and can apply this to their own lives.

For example, learners can write about what happened to the rich young ruler of Mark 10:17-22 after he turned away from Christ. Here are three other variations of story writing:

1. Open-ended stories

Start telling a story which involves decisions based on truths covered by the session or unit topic. Develop the story only far enough to reach the point where decisions must be made by the characters. Then allow the learners five to ten minutes to write an ending for the story.

These stories can be used in the same or in a later session as a dramatic activity (see Spontaneous Drama in Chapter 6).

2. Contemporary stories

Learners write a contemporary story about how some young people of their own age lived up to the lesson truths just studied.

Often by the end of a unit, learners can write a personal story about their own experiences in learning during the unit.

3. Parallel stories

Learners read a Bible story and analyze the feelings of the characters in the story and then identify the decisions facing those characters. Then learners write a story in a modern setting in which the characters have the same feelings as the Bible characters and are facing the same decisions.

For example, what might happen if Jesus walked into Washington, D.C. in the 1970s? Would the same things happen as happened in Jerusalem, almost two thousand years ago?

Unless stories are to be saved and used later in the unit as dramatic activities, stories are shared and discussed with the rest of the class during the session.

EXPLORING STORY WRITING POSSIBILITIES

Based on the session goals and the specific needs of the learners, story writing can be designed to:
1. Give life to Bible stories.
2. Relate Bible truths to today's life.
3. Share the feelings of biblical characters.
4. Compare events which happened in Bible times with today.

CHECKLIST OF MATERIALS NEEDED

_____ Lined paper
_____ Pencils
_____ Clear instructions

TV SCRIPT (B;7-12;L or S)

Learners read a Bible story and write it into a TV script. Or, learners write a script in a modern setting which shows biblically correct or incorrect behavior, and human characteristics.

DISCOVERING TV SCRIPTS

Almost any Bible study can be built around an assignment to write a TV script. If the script is a long one, the project carries over into the next session. The writing can be completed in one session and acted out the following week.

An effective TV script can be written on: "How would an evening news program cover the events of Judges 6,7?" The learners work in small groups with each group taking part of the total newscast: local news, weather, sports, national news, gossip, etc.

EXPLORING TV SCRIPT POSSIBILITIES

Based on the session goals, and the specific needs of the learners, TV scripts can help the learners to:

1. Identify with the Bible characters.
2. Know the session Scriptures well, as they decide which facts to include in the script.
3. Analyze a Bible story.
4. Summarize the main points of a story.

CHECKLIST OF MATERIALS NEEDED

_____ Lined paper
_____ Pencils
_____ Clear instructions

TESTS (B,C;7-12;L or S)

A test is a learning activity and an evaluative device.

There are several forms of tests. Individual learners or small groups of learners mark the correct answers to a test (multiple choice, true or false, or matching). Or, learners write in the correct words for the blanks in a given sentence. Some tests include essay questions.

DISCOVERING TESTS

Distribute survey tests at the beginning of a quarter or unit of study about the topics and information to be covered. Provide envelopes in which the learners seal their test papers. After the learners have written their names on the outside of the envelopes, collect them and hold them until the end of the unit. Then return the envelopes to the learners unopened and unread.

Test questions and the correct answers are usually discussed, but the learners' scores are usually kept confidential.

Creative testing techniques are discussed more thoroughly in Chapter 10, "Enjoy It!"

EXPLORING TEST POSSIBILITIES

Based on the session goals, and the specific needs of the learners, test can:

1. Summarize a unit or quarter.
2. Determine how much the learners know before or have learned during a unit of study.
3. Evaluate teaching effectiveness.

CHECKLIST OF MATERIALS NEEDED

_____ Lined paper
_____ Pencils
_____ Duplicated tests
and sometimes . . .
_____ Envelopes

WORD PUZZLES (A,B,C;7-12;L or S)

Creative word puzzles and games can make learning fun. Give the learners a copy of a word puzzle to be solved. Such puzzles can include jumbled names, a crossword puzzle, scrambled Bible verses, or a "Who-Am-I?" description.

DISCOVERING WORD PUZZLES

Word comparison is another type of word game. Learners read a passage in two or three different translations and then make up a chart showing the different words used to describe a person, an item, or the responses of the different characters in the story.

Jesus used word comparisons often, "Ye have said . . . but I say . . ." when comparing traditions with the real truth.

Word association is another variation. State the session topic in one or two words and ask the learners to quickly write down the first five or ten words and phrases which come to their minds. This activity helps learners think about the session subject.

Puzzles can be designed to require the learners to study and research the session Scriptures to find the answers. As learners share and discuss their answers to the puzzles, they also discuss the session topic and learn by the activity.

EXPLORING WORD PUZZLE POSSIBILITIES

Based on the session aims and the specific needs of the learners, word puzzles can help the learners to:
1. Explore the session topic.
2. Discover scriptural truths.
3. Enjoy learning.
4. Investigate variations of meanings in a passage.

CHECKLIST OF MATERIALS NEEDED

_____ Lined paper, 3"x5" cards, or duplicated word puzzle
_____ Pencils
_____ Bibles (possibly in several translations)
_____ Clear instructions

WRITING ACTIVITIES ARE SUCCESSFUL WHEN TEACHERS:

1. Assemble needed materials before the session.
2. Bring enough materials for a few extra learners.
3. Arrange the classroom before the session.
4. Remember that learning comes more often while working on the assignment rather than while reporting results.
5. Write out instructions whenever possible (on the chalkboard, a flipchart, or provide duplicated copies).
6. Allow enough time for the activity, and let the learners know how much time they have for the activity.
7. Encourage learners to use their imaginations.
8. Compliment good ideas, thoughts, completed assignments and group cooperation.

AND WHEN TEACHERS DO NOT:

1. Emphasize the use of perfect grammar, punctuation and spelling.
2. Put down the learners' ideas.
3. Expect learners always to agree with their ideas.

4. Compete with learners (in other words, it is perfectly acceptable to do a sample of the assignment before class and bring it to class to give the learners an idea of the format they could use for completing the assignment, but no clever "masterpieces" please!).
5. Embarrass learners whose writing ability is noticeably sub-standard by reading their compositions to the class. Instead, perhaps the teacher could list the main points they wrote about or give their good ideas.
6. Make up tests and quizzes which are too difficult or are only a test of rote memory.

YOUR NOTES: (Complete the following sentence.)

When I used writing activities . . .

CHAPTER SIX

DRAMATIZE IT!

Dramatic activities involve learners in acting out assigned or chosen roles as a learning experience.

USE DRAMATIC BIBLE LEARNING ACTIVITIES TO:

Empathize with the feelings of a biblical character;
Gain insight and understanding of the actions of others;
Understand one's self better.

Dramatic Bible Learning Activities can add sparkle and fun to almost any learning situation. Dramatic activities vary from spontaneous acting to the formal presentation of a play, including such experiences as roleplay, play reading and sociodrama.

Drama is popular with young people because it allows learners to express safely their own ideas and feelings by projecting them into a make-believe character.

Dramatic activities build strong group spirit, especially if the presentation requires the cast to rehearse once or twice before the presentation. Even spontaneous drama, however, can weld a group together.

Dramatic activities help learners gain insight and understanding on their own. Other teaching methods often require the teacher to point out a hidden truth. Bible characters suddenly come alive and become human beings to learn from instead of just being paper examples of good and bad behavior.

Dramatic presentations strongly reinforce what learning has taken place during the preparation period prior to the presentation.

The following chart indicates that dramatic Bible Learning Activities are effective channels for a teacher to meet the learners' spiritual needs while fulfilling each of their basic needs.

The scripts, unfinished stories or roleplay ideas used for dramatic Bible Learning Activities often can be produced from a creative writing assignment in a prior session. In this way one session builds on and is tied to another, developing a unit learning experience lasting several weeks.

Follow *each* of these activities with a group discussion or half of their value will be lost.

CONFLICT ROLES (A,B;10-12;L or S)

Conflict roles is a variation of the basic roleplay. (See Roleplay.)

DISCOVERING CONFLICT ROLES

Give conflicting role instructions to two or three class members. The roleplay characters approach a problem situation with opposing viewpoints.

Periodically, during the activity, hand one or more of the roleplayers new instructions which supercede all previous instructions.

The following example illustrates a lesson on Christian dating relationships:

Instructions No. 1 for Sally: You are driving home from the skating rink with Joe after your first date with him. You are beginning to like him very much—he's special somehow! Talk to Joe as you would in this situation. You are five miles from home.

Instructions for Joe: You are driving Sally home from the skating rink after your first date with her. Since you are only four blocks from her house right now, you are considering whether or not to kiss her goodnight. You do want to!

A DRAMATIC BIBLE LEARNING ACITIVTY

PHYSICAL	SECURITY	SOCIAL	SELF-RESPECT	ACHIEVEMENT	SPIRITUAL
—provides opportunities to move around —allows learners to relax from the traditional "sit still, shut up and listen" teaching techniques	—provides for use of skills and talents —allows groups to form and work together —provides a reachable goal —provides a variety of learning experiences —helps develop a good mental attitude	—allows conversation —encourages helping each other —provides fun and fellowship —builds friendships	—promotes understanding and acceptance —gives opportunities for recognition, praise and appreciation —develops self respect and respect for others as understanding increases	—provides a chance to fulfill one's capabilities —allows discovery of and use of one's potential —gets the stage for gaining insight and new knowledge	—removes fear barrier some people have about openly expressing their ideas —involves learners directly with the lesson truths or characters —illustrates a truth better than a lecture or sermon could —begins the integration of lesson truths into the lives of the learners —demonstrates what might happen in situations, and helps learners prepare for eventualities by coming to a solution in the make-believe situation —is a problem solving technique —allows practice in a nonthreatening atmosphere (Practice witnessing with each other, etc.) —generates discussion of God's truths

Instructions No. 2 for Sally: You are almost home now and beginning to wonder if Joe will kiss you goodnight. Do you want him to? In the car or at the door?

Instructions No. 3 for Sally: It looks like Joe is planning to kiss you in the car—he will probably get carried away. How are you going to discourage him, but still let him know that you like him?

EXPLORING CONFLICT ROLE POSSIBILITIES

Based on the session goals and the specific needs of the learners, conflict roles can help learners to:

1. Deal with daily frustrations by practicing in a classroom situation.
2. Delve beneath the surface situation and discover hidden personal needs.
3. Apply God's Word to life problems.
4. Explore alternative behavior in a frustrating circumstance.

CHECKLIST OF MATERIALS NEEDED

_____ Role-briefing sheets
(Character and problem descriptions and instructions)
_____ At least two sheets, changing the original instructions

FORMAL DRAMATIZATION (B,C;9-12;S-L)

A class of learners plan a play presentation for the rest of the department. They write the script, rehearse, draw backgrounds, collect props, design and duplicate programs and finally make the presentation.

DISCOVERING FORMAL DRAMATIZATIONS

The learners make a very large emotional investment in this kind of activity. Therefore, it is a powerful teacher. Much learning occurs if a teacher helps the learners to make a successful presentation.

The Bible is full of action stories which lend themselves to formal dramatizations.

EXPLORING FORMAL DRAMATIZATION POSSIBILITIES

Based on the session goals and the specific needs of the learners, formal dramatizations can be planned to:
1. Revitalize a familiar Bible story.
2. Explore a Bible character or story.
3. Share one's personal faith.
4. Portray the life of a famous missionary, or the frightening possibilities of a future and an eternity without Christ (e.g., *In the Twinkling of an Eye*).

CHECKLIST OF MATERIALS NEEDED

_____ Copies of the play script
_____ Props, costumes
_____ Sound effects, lights and music optional

PANTOMIME (A,B;7-9;S)

In pantomime, actions are exaggerated to convey a message which can be easily understood. The actors do not speak verbally.

DISCOVERING PANTOMIME

Give pantomime assignments written on small slips of paper to one or two volunteers in a small group. The volunteers act out the assignment for the rest of the group. The pantomime assignment may be to act out a situation or to just express a certain emotion. The rest of the group identifies and discusses the situation or emotion being portrayed.

The pantomime can be varied by having a cast of players silently walking through the motions of the story while a narrator reads the Bible story, or a script.

EXPLORING PANTOMIME POSSIBILITIES

Based on the session goals and the specific needs of the learners, pantomimes might help learners:
1. Become familiar with the feelings of the Bible characters.
2. Express their concepts of a biblical character's behavior and emotions.

3. Identify and discuss behavior patterns and problems unbecoming to a believer.
4. Discover life changes they need to make.

CHECKLIST OF MATERIALS NEEDED

_____ Pantomime assignments

and sometimes . . .

_____ A Bible, contemporary, or missionary story, or a play to be read by the teacher to the learners

PLAY READING (B,C;7-8;L or S)

Reading aloud the script of a short, well-written play is a learning activity requiring minimal preparation time.

Briefly explain the setting and the important truths of the play to the entire group.

Either assign or give out the various parts in the script on a volunteer basis. Give each reader a copy of the script.

The learners who read the play to the others sit facing the rest of the group.

Play reading is best used as a small group activity, so that each learner in the group can participate. A circular seating arrangement lends itself well to this activity.

EXPLORING PLAY READING POSSIBILITIES

Based on the session goals and the specific needs of the learners, play reading might be used to:
1. Familiarize learners with the lesson truths.
2. Reinforce the unit theme and goal.
3. Illustrate the central point of the lesson.

CHECKLIST OF MATERIALS NEEDED

_____ Copies of the play script.

PUPPETS (C;7-12;L)

Hand puppets and marionettes can help students of all ages learn.

Give puppets to two or three learners who then go to the front of the class for an impromptu drama. Learners conduct roleplay situation or act out the end of a spontaneous dramatic situation for the others.

Puppets sometimes "say" things which the learners do not feel free to say as themselves.

EXPLORING PUPPET POSSIBILITIES

Based on the session goals and the specific needs of the learners puppets can be a way to:
1. Summarize or demonstrate the session truths.
2. Explore the personal implications of the session.

CHECKLIST OF MATERIALS NEEDED

_____ Puppets (hand or marionettes)
_____ Role briefing sheets, short play script, or unfinished story
_____ Clear instructions

ROLEPLAY (A,B,C;10-12;L or S)

A roleplay is acting out a common situation which involves decisions based on the session truths.

DISCOVERING ROLEPLAYS

Distribute a role briefing sheet which describes a problem situation involving two to five learners. Only one of the characters involved in the given situation is described on the sheet. A roleplay differs slightly from spontaneous drama in that in a roleplay the learners are told to behave in a specific way, i.e., selfishly, irritatingly or cheerfully.

The learners have five minutes to study their roles before they act out the problem situation described.

The roleplay continues until a solution is found or until the announced time limit is reached.

Sometimes the learners observing the roleplay activity achieve insight from the Holy Spirit as they see themselves in the roles being played by their classmates.

Of course, specific biblical answers need to be found

for the problem during the discussion which follows the roleplay.

EXPLORING ROLEPLAY POSSIBILITIES

Based on the session goals and the specific needs of the learners, roleplays can be designed to:
1. Familiarize learners with session concepts.
2. Explore or illustrate scriptural truths.
3. Draw out personal feelings and ideas about the session Scripture.
4. Indicate the learner's level of understanding.

CHECKLIST OF MATERIALS NEEDED

_____ Role briefing sheets (a different one for each character in the roleplay) which give a brief outline of the roleplay situation, and a description of the character to be played with instructions about the emotional and mental state of the character

_____ Clear instructions

SILENT FILM SCRIPTING (B,C;7-10;S-L)

Writing the script for their own film helps young people learn Bible truth.

DISCOVERING SILENT FILM SCRIPTING

A small group of learners plan a movie to depict a Bible theme, contemporary story or a documentary. They write the script and make the movie. When the film is processed, a presentation is made to the entire group.

Writing the script is the part of the project where most of the learning occurs. Do not write the script for the learners!

EXPLORING SILENT FILM SCRIPTING POSSIBILITIES

Based on the session goals and the specific needs of the learners, silent film scripting can:
1. Portray little known historical events surrounding a biblical event.

2. Deepen the learners' understanding of a unit theme being illustrated by the movie.

CHECKLIST OF MATERIALS NEEDED

___ Movie camera
___ Film
___ Projector
___ Projection screen
___ Lined paper
___ Pencils
___ Clear instructions

SKIT (A,B,C;7-12;S-L)

A skit is similar to a roleplay in that it is a very short presentation designed to illustrate one basic biblical truth. A skit, however, follows a script and the participants do memorize their lines before the presentation.

DISCOVERING SKITS

A script enables specific statements to be included for discussion after the skit.

EXPLORING SKIT POSSIBILITIES

Based on the session goals and the specific needs of the learners, skits:

Introduce, explore, illustrate or summarize the session truths.

CHECKLIST OF MATERIALS NEEDED

___ Copies of the skit script
___ Clear instructions

SLIDE SHOW (B,C;7-12;S-L)

A small group of learners plan a series of pictures which illustrate a Bible story, a song, a theme, or the learners make up a story or documentary and illustrate it with slides.

DISCOVERING SLIDE SHOWS

Working with the teacher, the learners take the pictures during the week and when the film is processed give a presentation during the class session.

Slide shows enable you and your learners to work together in an exciting context. But the learners will not learn much if you try to run the show! The learners must be free to learn as they do!

A slide show is an excellent unit closing activity. The preparation ties several sessions together with a continuous project.

EXPLORING SLIDE SHOW POSSIBILITIES

Based on the session goals and the specific needs of the learners, a slide show can:

Introduce, explore, illustrate or summarize the unit truths.

CHECKLIST OF MATERIALS NEEDED

_____ Slide camera
_____ Film
_____ Projector
_____ Projector screen
_____ Clear instructions

SLIDE-TAPE SHOW (B,C;7-12;S-L)

A small group of learners plan a slide show as described earlier but add a recorded narration and music to complete the presentation.

DISCOVERING SLIDE-TAPE SHOWS

For example, a slide and tape show on "The Christian's Joy" can be a series of slides showing smiles and happy faces—adults in a crowd, children at play, a mother smiling at her baby! The tape can include hymns as well as songs that are current and popular with the learners, and Bible verses like John 15:9-11 and 16:23,24.

EXPLORING SLIDE-TAPE SHOW POSSIBILITIES

Based on the session goals and the specific needs of the learners a slide-tape show can:

Introduce, explore, illustrate or summarize the unit truths.

CHECKLIST OF MATERIALS NEEDED

_____ Same as for suggestion for slide show
_____ Tape recorder and microphone
_____ Tape
_____ Lined paper
_____ Pencils
_____ Clear instructions

SOCIODRAMA (C;11-12;S)

Learners having real-life problems which relate to one of the truths presented in a lesson contribute their problem to the class.

DISCOVERING SOCIODRAMA

Learners briefly explain the problem and then act out their own part in the situation with one or two of the other learners playing the part of the other people involved in the problem (overly strict parents, for example). Biblical answers to the problems discussed are shared with the learners. Sociodrama is very much like roleplay, only the number of learners participating is expanded. You can reverse the roles of the learners and redo the sociodrama for additional insights into the problem.

EXPLORING SOCIODRAMA POSSIBILITIES

Based on the session aims, and the specific needs of the learners, sociodrama can be used to:
1. Help learners get suggestions for changing their own behavior to help them cope with their problems.
2. Give personal insight to the learners.
3. Draw a unit or session to a logical and profitable close.

CHECKLIST OF MATERIALS NEEDED

_____ Learners who are willing to share one of their own real-life problems with the others

SPONTANEOUS DRAMA (A,C;9-12;L)

Spontaneous, or impromptu drama requires no preparation by the learners and thus makes a great introductory or closing activity.

DISCOVERING SPONTANEOUS DRAMA

Ask two or three learners to volunteer to act out an ending to an unfinished story. Read the background and setting of the story to the entire group. Then without any planning, ask the volunteers to act out an ending for the story based on what they think might happen in real life if the story were true.

The situation can be a continuation of a Bible story or a modern-day situation applying the principles of the Bible lesson of the week.

For example: suppose the group has just finished studying about the man beside the Bethesda pool who had been ill for thirty-eight years before Jesus healed him. The learners can be helped to understand the responses of others not involved in the miracle and the realities the man would be facing, by having the learners do a spontaneous drama of that man interviewing for a job one week after he had been healed. Explain that the man had not worked for thirty-eight years, may not have had any skills, and probably did not have any personal references, because the Pharisees were angry with him for carrying his bed on the Sabbath!

Ask one learner to be the healed man and one or two others to be merchants. The learners take the story from there, making up the lines as they go.

While watching the spontaneous drama, you and the other learners listen for honest opinions, cliches, insight to dialogues at home and for veiled cries for help.

EXPLORING SPONTANEOUS DRAMA POSSIBILITIES

Based on the session aims and the specific needs of the learners, a teacher might use drama to:
1. Introduce, explore or demonstrate the session Scripture.
2. Revitalize a familiar Bible story, in order to discover new implications for life in today's world.

CHECKLIST OF MATERIALS NEEDED

_____ An unfinished story—usually two or three short paragraphs, developed just far enough to involve the characters in a problem situation which requires decisions based on the session truths
_____ Clear instructions
_____Learners who are expressive

TABLEAU (A,B;7-8;L or S)

A tableau is a stylized form of acting out a story during a narration.

DISCOVERING TABLEAUX

Direct a group of learners to assume the posture and placement of the people in a specific scene in a Bible story. Once they have assumed the correct pose, the learners do not move nor speak while you read the events of the scene.

Either the same cast poses the next scene or a new cast may come to the front of the room and pose the scene.

A tableau helps learners visualize a Bible story such as Ruth and Boaz or David hiding from Saul. Scenic backdrops and simple props may enhance a tableau activity, but are not essential to its success.

EXPLORING TABLEAU POSSIBILITIES

Based on the session goals and the specific needs of the learners, a tableau may:

1. Explore a Bible character or story.
2. Revitalize a familiar Bible story.
3. Help visualize unfamiliar scenes.

CHECKLIST OF MATERIALS NEEDED

_____ Bible Story or play script to be read by the teacher to the class
_____ Props, costumes, backdrops, lights and music are optional
_____ Clear instructions

TV FORMAT ON BIBLE TRUTHS (A,B,C;7-12;S-L)

A television format offers several options as a Bible Learning Activity.

DISCOVERING TV FORMAT

Probably the easiest and yet the most versatile method for acquainting learners with Bible truths is the TV newscast. (See Chapter 5, "TV Script" for added details.)

Other TV formats can be devised by having the learners work together in two groups planning a quiz show presentation. One group makes up questions to ask the other group about a Scripture passage. Meanwhile the second group studies the Scripture passage while trying to anticipate what questions they will be asked.

After a few minutes, the two groups are reassembled and the quiz begins.

There have been several TV formats which are adaptable to Bible learning, including: "Password," "Jeopardy," "Concentration," "Call My Bluff," "It's Your Bet," "This Is Your Life . . . ," "You Don't Say," "To Tell the Truth," and "What's My Line?"

This activity can be used as a creative testing activity at the end of the session or a unit of study or a quarter. You can elect to prepare the test questions to use before the session.

EXPLORING TV FORMAT POSSIBILITIES

Based on the session goals and the specific needs of the learners, TV Format can:
1. Introduce, explore or summarize the session truths.
2. Evaluate the teacher's effectiveness.
3. Determine the level of learner understanding of the session or unit truths.

CHECKLIST OF MATERIALS NEEDED

____ Lined paper
____ Pencils
____ Clear instructions
____ You may want to add some props to create the "right" atmosphere.

DRAMATIC ACTIVITIES ARE SUCCESSFUL WHEN TEACHERS:

1. Assemble needed supplies before class, always bringing enough for a few extra learners who may be present.
2. Set up the room before the session.
3. Duplicate copies of the scripts to be used.
4. Show enthusiasm.
5. Enter into the spirit of the activity.
6. Compliment learners on their participation.
7. Encourage the audience to listen by giving them listening assignments before any presentation.
8. Remember that form and perfection are not half as important as the content and the learning experience.

AND WHEN TEACHERS DO NOT:

1. Act out a role themselves unless absolutely necessary.
2. Allow learners to make fun of each other's acting.
3. Try to inhibit learners' expressions of feeling, etc.

YOUR NOTES: (Complete the following sentence.)

When I used dramatic activities . . .

CHAPTER SEVEN

DRAW IT!

Art is any pictorial, graphic or symbolic expression of a theme, a story, a feeling or an idea including paintings, doodlings, drawings and designs.

USE ART BIBLE LEARNING ACTIVITIES TO:

Capture the interest and stimulate the imagination of the learners by allowing creative, nonverbal expression of ideas;
Make Bible learning fun;
Help learners visualize truths.

A desire for self-expression is a common feeling among today's youth. You can capitalize on that desire by using art as a Bible Learning Activity in the classroom.

An interesting art activity appeals to that inner creative self God has given each human being. Learners who shudder at the sight of a pencil, lined paper and the thought of a writing assignment, may eagerly reach for a sheet of drawing paper and a paintbrush or felt-tip pen.

Art activities can tie all the sessions of a unit together by leaving the completed projects from the various sessions on display in the classroom for the duration of the unit. All previous art projects should be removed from the room at the beginning of a new unit of study, however.

Your unwillingness to use unfamiliar art activities deprives your learners of many enjoyable and profitable

AN ART BIBLE LEARNING ACTIVITY

PHYSICAL	SECURITY	SOCIAL	SELF-RESPECT	ACHIEVEMENT	SPIRITUAL
—provides opportunity to move around —is asthetically pleasing when used in the room as part of the decor	—provides experiences —uses skills and talents —allows team work	—provides fellowship with friends while working in groups —allows conversation —encourages helping each other	—invites recognition, attention, appreciation, and praise —provides avenues for understanding and accepting one another's ideas	—provides opportunities for using one's abilities —encourages individual thought and ideas, as well as creativity and imagination	—provides means for teacher to check understanding of the learners —involves learners in the events of the lesson or with the lesson theme —allows for insight and inspiration from God while trying to understand a lesson well enough to express ideas about the lesson in an art project —often causes learners to analyze lesson passages more carefully than they would otherwise

learning experiences. Art activities can direct learners' attention to Bible truths while fulfilling each of their basic needs. How they do this is shown on the preceding chart:

The following ideas are samples of the hundreds of ways art can be used in the classroom. They are only guidelines. Adapt these suggestions to your session and to your own particular learners.

Decide whether displaying a project or taking it home as a reminder of the lesson adds the most to the learning value of the assignment.

Most of the following suggestions may be adapted to become either individual or small group assignments depending on whether you plan to follow the art activity with small or large group discussion.

ADVERTISEMENT BROCHURE (A,B,C;7-12;L or S)

Ask learners to make up a brochure advertising themselves, some phase of Christianity, Christ or a Bible character.

DISCOVERING ADVERTISING BROCHURES

As an *Approach* activity learners can show how much they already know about the session character or topic by roughing out ideas for a brochure. Details for the brochure are verified and supplemented during the Bible Study phase of the session. As a summarizing activity, brochures are made during the *Conclusion and Decision* phase of the session.

Share and discuss the brochures. Display is optional.

EXPLORING ADVERTISEMENT BROCHURE POSSIBILITIES

Based on the session goals and the specific needs of the learners, brochures can:
1. Introduce, explore or summarize the main points of the session or unit.
2. Illustrate learners' concepts and indicate areas of learning needs.

CHECKLIST OF MATERIALS NEEDED
_____ Colorful paper
_____ Felt-tip pens

_____ Collage material (magazines, newspapers, cata-
logues, etc.)
_____ Scissors
_____ Tape or glue
_____ Clear instructions

BANNERS (A,C;7-10;S)

A banner can be a symbolic flag or a long, narrow "sign"
such as those which are stretched above city streets
to announce such activities as "Pioneer Week" or special events.

DISCOVERING BANNERS

Learners work in small groups to design and make banners. A typical assignment might be to design a banner
which could have been carried by one of the Bible kings,
or a banner for the apostles, or even a banner Christians
could claim.

Banners painted on butcher paper are a quick but
effective *Approach* activity for the first session of a new
unit.

More elaborate banners made of felt or burlap can
be a continuing project over a period of more than one
class session.

Share and discuss the completed banners in small
groups. Display is recommended.

EXPLORING BANNER POSSIBILITIES

Based on the session goals and the specific needs of
the learners, banners could be planned to:
1. Relate session truths to a believer's life today.
2. Analyze the main characteristics of the session
   personality.
3. Introduce or summarize the central truths of a
   session or unit.

CHECKLIST OF MATERIALS NEEDED

_____ Large sheets of paper, or butcher paper
_____ Felt-tip pens or paints and brushes
_____ Scissors

_____ Clear instructions

and sometimes . . .

_____ Felt squares (at least 12"x12") in various colors
_____ Burlap in various colors
_____ White glue
_____ Oil paints and brushes

BOOK COVERS (A,B,C;7-10;L)

Creating book covers activates the learners' imaginations and results in a most interesting art display.

DISCOVERING BOOK COVERS

Ask each learner to design an attractive and informative book cover which would be appropriate for a biography of a Bible character or maybe of themselves. Learners include the usual plot summary and "selected quotes" on the inside flaps of the book covers.

After sharing and discussing his project, each learner puts the completed book cover on a book and displays it on a table at one side of the classroom.

The real Bible learning in this activity takes place when each learner researches the biography of a Bible character in order to design his book cover.

EXPLORING BOOK COVER POSSIBILITIES

Based on the session goals and the specific needs of the learners, book covers can help learners to:
1. Become familiar with the session character.
2. Investigate the Scriptures to find specific facts for their project.
3. Discover, explore or summarize the session truths in relation to their own personal life situation.

CHECKLIST OF MATERIALS NEEDED

_____ Large sheets of drawing paper
_____ Colored felt-tip pens
_____ A hardback book for each learner (a hymnbook works well!)
_____ Clear instructions

BUMPER STICKERS OR CAMPAIGN BADGES (A,C;7-10;S-L)

Small groups work together designing and making "campaign badges" or bumper stickers which summarize the session theme.

DISCOVERING BUMPER STICKERS

Learners enjoy summarizing their ideas about the session or unit theme into catchy or meaningful slogans.
For example: "All the Bible says is true. Don't shine it on!"
"There are no equivalent measures with God!"
"Christianity is dependable: Wear it with confidence!"
"God's Word is so complete, all you add is love!"
A representative from each group shares the groups' projects with the other learners. Display is recommended.

EXPLORING BUMPER STICKER POSSIBILITIES

Based on the session goals and the specific needs of the learners, bumper stickers can:
1. Introduce the session or unit topic, or biblical character to be studied.
2. Summarize the learning of the unit.

CHECKLIST OF MATERIALS NEEDED

_____ Adhesive contact paper (several plain colors)
_____ Scissors
_____ Rulers
___ Pencils
_____ Alphabet stencil
_____ Clear instructions

CARTOON STRIP (B,C;7-10;S or S-L)

A cartoon sequence of three to eight pictures is a learning experience in which class members research and discuss the session Scripture to discover the main points to include in the cartoon strip.

DISCOVERING CARTOON STRIPS

Each learner divides his paper into no more than eight

sections and illustrates the events of a Bible story. These cartoon strips are then shared and discussed in small groups.

The parables Jesus told are fun to illustrate with a cartoon strip activity.

Each cartoon strip is shared and discussed with the rest of the learners. Display is optional.

EXPLORING CARTOON STRIP POSSIBILITIES

Based on the session aims and the specific needs of the learners, cartoon strips can be designed to:
1. Explore the details of the session Scripture.
2. Compare two similar Bible stories or parables.
3. Illustrate the session Scripture.

CHECKLIST OF MATERIALS NEEDED

_____ Sheets of drawing paper (at least 8½"x11")
_____ Pencils, colored felt-tip pens
_____ Clear instructions

COAT OF ARMS (A,B,C;7-9;L or S)

A coat of arms is a shield with a personal insignia on it, or a representation of such a shield.

DISCOVERING COATS OF ARMS

After displaying a picture of a traditional coat of arms, each learner creates a Christian coat of arms for himself, a Bible character, or for Christ.

This is a good introductory activity for a unit of study on one particular Bible character.

The learners' coat of arms are shared and discussed. Display is recommended.

EXPLORING COAT OF ARMS POSSIBILITIES

Based on the session aims and the specific needs of the learners, the teacher might plan a coat-of-arms activity to:
1. Familiarize the learners with the session truths or character.
2. Obtain learner feedback on the study.

3. Explore or summarize the session Scripture.

CHECKLIST OF MATERIALS NEEDED

_____ Large sheets of drawing paper
_____ Felt-tip pens (various colors)
_____ Sample drawing of a coat of arms
_____ Clear instructions

COLLABORATIVE DRAWINGS (C;7-12;S-L)

Learners work together on a drawing which illustrates Bible truth.

DISCOVERING COLLABORATIVE DRAWINGS

Diads collaborate on a drawing illustrating one particular event covered in the session. The pair works together without any verbal communication, hence without discussing or planning the drawing.

When they are finished, each pair discusses their drawings and then shares it with the others. Display is optional.

Learners then share and discuss these composite drawings.

EXPLORING COLLABORATIVE DRAWING POSSIBILITIES

Based on the session goals and the specific needs of the learners, these drawings can help learners to:
1. Express their understanding of the sessions's central truth.
2. Respond to the session Scripture.
3. Summarize or illustrate the session.

CHECKLIST OF MATERIALS NEEDED

_____ Large sheets of drawing paper
_____ Pencils or felt-tip pens
_____ Clear instructions

COLLAGE/MONTAGE (A,C;7-12;S)

A collage or montage is a composite representation of a theme or idea. A montage is a picture made by combining several pictures or words. A collage includes printed matter and the other materials creating a three-dimension effect.

DISCOVERING COLLAGES AND MONTAGES

Learners work in small groups to create a collage or montage which elaborates on a theme or conveys a message. A separate set of materials is given to each group.

The assignment is completed by cutting out words, slogans and pictures from the magazines and gluing the cutouts on a poster board. A collage might include buttons, beads, pine cones or other materials.

For example, after a study of Romans 8, one small group creates a montage depicting "the natural man". Another small group depicts "the spiritual man".

Collages or montages are shared and discussed with the other learners. Display is optional.

EXPLORING COLLAGE AND MONTAGE POSSIBILITIES

Based on the session aims and the specific needs of the learners, collages or montages can help learners:
1. Become familiar with, explore or summarize the central truth of the session or unit.
2. Express their personal feelings, opinions or ideas.

CHECKLIST OF MATERIALS NEEDED

_____ Colored construction paper or poster board
_____ Materials (old magazines, newspapers, catalogues, buttons, string, seeds, etc.)
_____ Scissors
_____ White glue, tape or a stapler and staples
_____ Clear instructions

DISPLAYS AND EXHIBITS (A,B,C;7-12;L or S)

All of the learners help prepare a display or exhibit illustrating a completed unit of study. Some learners can work individually on part of the display while others work in small groups on the other parts. Displays can include any type of art project! The teacher and the learners use their imaginations and go creative!!!

DISCOVERING DISPLAYS

The entire class time for the last session of a unit of study can be used for creating a display or exhibit.

Or, a display can be a continuing project throughout the unit with portions of each session devoted to preparing the display.

Each part of the completed display is explained to the others by the learners who worked on that part. Parents or learners from other departments can be invited to come and see the completed display or exhibit after the session.

EXPLORING DISPLAY POSSIBILITIES

Based on the session aims and the specific needs of the learners, displays can help learners to:
1. Understand the overall unit theme.
2. Share what they have learned with others.
3. Express their personal faith.

CHECKLIST OF MATERIALS NEEDED

_____ Completed projects from all sessions in the unit (art, writing, music, research, reports, etc.)

_____ Supplemental art materials as needed (poster board, cutouts, scissors, glue, crepe paper, felt-tip pens, etc.)

_____ Clear instructions

DOODLES (A,C;7-12;L or S)

Doodles differ from drawings in that they are not the result of an attempt to draw an accurate picture.

DISCOVERING DOODLES

Suggest that each learner do a doodle while listening to a recording. After the recording is finished, the learners share and discuss three things:
1. What they heard.
2. Their honest response to what they heard.

3. Their doodles.

You can gain a great deal of insight into your learners' thoughts through this art activity and the discussion. Doodling helps learners focus on and define their feelings, providing effective feedback which might otherwise be lost.

Display is not recommended—doodles out of the lesson and discussion context may seem humorous to anyone coming into the classroom after the session and hence a learning activity could become an embarrassment for the learners.

EXPLORING DOODLE POSSIBILITIES

Based on the session goals and the specific needs of the learners, doodles can be used to:
1. Surface learner response to a presentation or to the topic being discussed.
2. Identify personal ideas and feelings of the learners.
3. Summarize the learning which has occurred during the session.

CHECKLIST OF MATERIALS NEEDED

_____ Drawing paper
_____ Pencils
_____ Encouragement and clear instructions

GRAFFITI POSTER (A;7-12;L or S)

A graffiti poster represents the many different ideas and opinions of the class members about an assigned topic.

DISCOVERING GRAFFITI

Before the session tape a large sheet of paper to the wall and write a topic across the top. As each learner enters the classroom he begins writing words and phrases or drawing pictures which might have been written or drawn on a city or building wall by people living at the time of the session's Bible story.

Graffiti is also a good way to draw out idea stereotypes, prejudices and concept definitions. Write the topic on the paper as an unfinished sentence such as: "Discipline is . . ."; "Love is . . ."; "War is . . ."; "Growing up is . . ."; "Prejudice is . . ."

This activity is an excellent way to involve immediately the learners with the session subject as soon as they enter the room.

EXPLORING GRAFFITI POSTER POSSIBILITIES

Based on the session goals and the specific needs of the learners, graffiti posters can:

1. Introduce and generate discussion of the session Scripture.
2. Draw out and define the personal opinions and ideas of the learners.
3. Involve learners with the session character as they imagine what he might have written.

CHECKLIST OF MATERIALS NEEDED

____ Very large sheet of drawing paper (or poster board; or roll of butcher paper)
____ Pencils or grease pencils
____ Clear instructions

GRAPHS (A,C;7-12;S or L)

There are various forms of graphs and charts used to help visualize a concept. Creative graphs enhance the classroom learning and help learners apply the lesson to their lives.

DISCOVERING GRAPHS

Ask the learners to illustrate various statistics or facts on a graph so they can visualize the relationships between two or more items.

For example, learners can evaluate their Christian lives, show how they spend their time or how they budget their money on a circle (or pie) chart.

Graphs are shared and discussed. Display is optional. The learners can benefit if some graphs are displayed on his bedroom wall as a daily reminder that some life changes are needed!

EXPLORING GRAPH POSSIBILITIES

Based on the session aims and the specific needs of each learner, graphs can be designed to:

1. Compare the characteristics of two biblical personalities or of the learners and the session personality.
2. Rate learners' behavior as compared to the ideas explained in God's Word.
3. Illustrate personal goals of the learners.
4. Analyze and explore the session Scriptures.

CHECKLIST OF MATERIALS NEEDED

_____ Paper (plain or graph)
_____ Pencils
_____ Rulers
_____ Clear instructions

MAPS (B,C;7-12;L or S)

Maps vary from simple line drawings to researched relief maps showing the mountains and valleys of a specific area.

DISCOVERING MAPS

Learners work individually or in small groups drawing maps. These maps may be the geographical setting for a Bible story, or symbolic maps illustrating something like "The Road from Unbelief to Belief."

Maps are shared and discussed. Display is recommended.

EXPLORING MAP POSSIBILITIES

Based on the session goals and the specific needs of the learners, maps can be used to:

Explore or illustrate the session Bible story, or truths.

CHECKLIST OF MATERIALS NEEDED

_____ Large sheets of drawing paper (or a roll of butcher paper)
_____ Pencils or felt-tip pens
_____ Clear instructions

MOBILES (A,C;7-12;S)

A mobile is an abstract paper sculpture made of several independent pieces, held together and tied to a ceiling beam or light fixture, etc., by heavy thread.

DISCOVERING MOBILES

A mobile can illustrate a unit, a session, an idea or an emotion. Small groups of learners cut out figures which symbolize the idea they want to convey. The cutouts are then attached to each other with thread, balanced, and then hung for display and explanation.

A mobile of the fruits of the Spirit is an example.

EXPLORING MOBILE POSSIBILITIES

Based on the session aims and the specific needs of the learners, mobiles can be planned to:

1. Familiarize learners with, review, or summarize the central truth of the session or unit.
2. Demonstrate the interrelationships of various concepts, through the use of symbols and designs.

CHECKLIST OF MATERIALS NEEDED

_____ Heavy card stock (various colors)
_____ Dark thread
_____ Plastic straws
_____ Scissors
_____ White glue
_____ Mobile pattern is optional
_____ Clear instructions

MURALS, DRAWINGS or PAINTINGS (C;7-12;L or S)

Working in small groups, learners illustrate the session idea, events or implications on a large drawing.

DISCOVERING MURALS

Murals, drawings and paintings are effective in involving artistic young people in Bible learning.

Projects are shared, discussed and displayed for the duration of the unit.

EXPLORING MURAL POSSIBILITIES

Based on the session goals and the specific needs of the learners, murals can help learners:
1. Understand the sequence of events covered in the unit and grasp the total picture and main points of the unit.
2. Illustrate the session Scripture.

CHECKLIST OF MATERIALS NEEDED

_____ Large sheet of paper (or a roll of butcher paper)
_____ Pencils or felt-tip pens
_____ Clear instructions

REBUS (B;7-9;L or S)

A rebus is a picture or symbol communication which substitutes pictures for words whenever possible.

DISCOVERING A REBUS

Learners work with a Scripture passage and substitute a symbol or picture for every word they can. Learners can work individually or in small groups.

Each rebus is shared and discussed. Display is recommended.

EXPLORING REBUS POSSIBILITIES

Based on the session goals and the specific needs of the learners, a rebus can help learners:
1. Explore the session Scripture for word meanings and implications.
2. Visualize the ideas of the session Scripture.

CHECKLIST OF MATERIALS NEEDED

_____ Large sheets of paper (or a roll of butcher paper)
_____ Pencils or felt-tip pens
_____ Clear instructions

ROAD OF LIFE (B,C;7-12;L or S)

A road of life is a line drawing which represents a series of events over a period of time.

DISCOVERING ROAD OF LIFE DRAWINGS

Ask each learner to place a dot on the left side of a sheet of paper. This dot represents his Christian birth. Then without lifting his pencil from the paper, he draws a line up or down and across the paper representing critical incidents in his Christian life.

Learners can draw a second road of life for a contemporary Christian leader, a famous missionary, or a Bible character. For instance, a study of the life of Jeremiah, Gideon or Elijah will show interesting highs and lows. The learner can then compare his own confidence in or love for God with that of Gideon, Elijah or Paul.

The drawings are shared and discussed during the session. Display is optional.

EXPLORING ROAD OF LIFE POSSIBILITIES

Based on the session aims and the specific needs of the learners, this type of drawing can help learners to:
1. Get an overall picture of their life style.
2. Notice life changes which should be made.
3. Discover similarities between themselves and the session characters.

CHECKLIST OF MATERIALS NEEDED

_____ Large sheets of drawing paper
_____ Pencils
_____ Clear instructions

SILHOUETTES (A,C;7-12;S-L)

Learners stand next to a large piece of butcher paper which is hung on a wall and have their classmates draw around them to obtain a life-size silhouette. Silhouettes are cut out and displayed.

DISCOVERING SILHOUETTES

The learners form diads and take turns drawing full-sized

silhouettes of each other. Silhouettes are then hung on the wall, and each one is given the name of a Bible character from the current unit of study.

All the learners walk around the room and write words and phrases which describe or relate to that character on each of the silhouettes, and read what the other learners have written.

This activity could be an effective review at the end of a unit on the disciples of Jesus or the kings of Judah and Israel.

EXPLORING SILHOUETTE POSSIBILITIES

Based on the session aims and the specific needs of the learners, silhouettes can be planned to:
1. Introduce, explore or summarize a session or unit of study.
2. Analyze the session character, based on biblical references to him.

CHECKLIST OF MATERIALS NEEDED

_____ A roll of butcher paper
_____ Pencils or grease pencils
_____ Scissors
_____ Masking tape
_____ Clear instructions

SKETCHES (A;7-12;L or S)

A sketch is a simple drawing, designed to express an idea or opinion.

DISCOVERING SKETCHES

Ask learners to express their understanding of a concept or idea in a sketch. For example, start a session by saying, "Today we're going to study prayer. I'd like you each to draw a picture of your idea of prayer. You have five minutes. OK? Go!" At first, learners may find it difficult to sketch an idea or opinion. A suggestion or two should start their creative processes working.

Sketches are shared and briefly discussed as a lead-in or approach to the session. Display is optional.

EXPLORING SKETCH POSSIBILITIES

Based on the session goals and the specific needs of the learners, sketches can:

1. Introduce the session topic.
2. Define learner response to the session concepts.

CHECKLIST OF MATERIALS NEEDED

____ Large sheets of drawing paper
____ Pencils
____ Clear instructions

SYMBOL DESIGN (A,C;9-12;S)

Learners use their imaginations to communicate a concept through an original design (e.g., the ecology symbol). Older young people handle this type of art activity better than seventh or eighth graders.

DISCOVERING SYMBOL DESIGN

Learners design a symbol of an assigned abstract characteristic such as one of the attributes of God, one of the fruits of the Spirit, or one of the spiritual benefits given to believers.

Learners work on the symbols as individuals, but share and discuss the finished symbol in small groups. The symbol might be used as a "clue" to a Bible story and the other learners could try to guess which story, parable or passage is being represented.

EXPLORING SYMBOL DESIGN POSSIBILITIES

Based on the session goals and the specific needs of the learners, symbol design might be assigned to:

Introduce, explore, or summarize the main idea of the session or unit.

CHECKLIST OF MATERIALS NEEDED

____ Drawing paper
____ Pencils
____ Clear instructions

WIRE EXPRESSIONS (A,C;7-12;S)

Wire expressions are similar to symbol designs, except that the symbols are three dimensional and done with wire.

DISCOVERING WIRE EXPRESSION

Give each learner one or more chenille-covered wires and direct him to symbolize a relationship, an idea, a Bible truth, or an attitude with the wires. Each learner then shares and discusses his symbol with the others in his small group. Display is optional.

EXPLORING WIRE EXPRESSION POSSIBILITIES

Based on the session goals and the specific needs of the learners, wire expressions could be planned to:
Introduce, explore, or summarize the session or unit theme.

CHECKLIST OF MATERIALS NEEDED

_____ Chenille-covered wires (preferably in several colors)
_____ Scissors
_____ Clear instructions

WORD PICTURES (A,B,C;9-12;S-L)

Words and phrases cut out from magazines or newspapers and glued to a poster board make a description or a word picture.

DISCOVERING WORD PICTURES

Learners work in small groups cutting words and phrases relating to an assigned theme. These words are then pasted onto a large sheet of drawing paper or poster board in such a way as to form a picture or symbol. Each learner interprets the word picture for the rest of the learners and the word pictures are displayed. Later the learners walk around the room reading each of the word pictures.

Meaning is conveyed not only by the words pasted on the poster board, but also by the arrangement of the words on the poster. A word picture of Jesus, for example, can have the words arranged to form a cross. A word picture of Christian characteristics might be arranged to form a dove or form the outline of a body to represent the body of Christ.

EXPLORING WORD PICTURE POSSIBILITIES

Based on the session aims and specific needs of the learners, word pictures can:

Introduce, explore, illustrate, or summarize the central truths of the session or unit.

CHECKLIST OF MATERIALS NEEDED

____ Poster board, or large sheets of drawing paper
____ Old magazines and newspapers
____ Scissors
____ White glue or tape
____ Clear instructions

ART ACTIVITIES ARE SUCCESSFUL WHEN TEACHERS:

1. Assemble needed materials before class, always bringing enough for a few extra learners who may be present.
2. Set up the room before the session.
3. Allow enough time to complete assignments.
4. Encourage 100 percent class participation.
5. Display the projects whenever profitable to the learners.
6. Have worktables if possible.
7. Compliment the learners on their work.
8. Expect and allow for more informal conversation than usual; teach conversationally by joining the conversations.
9. Allow learners to share and discuss their work.

AND WHEN TEACHERS DO NOT:

1. Make the projects for the learners.
2. Force their ideas on the learners.
3. Allow learners to make fun of any attempted projects.
4. Expect masterpieces.
5. Forget to clean up the room promptly after the session.

YOUR NOTES: (Complete this sentence.)

When I used art activities . . .

CHAPTER EIGHT

SING IT!

Music related activities involve learners in studying or composing songs.

USE MUSIC BIBLE LEARNING ACTIVITIES TO:

Teach Bible truth.
Explore the meaning and place of music in learning.
Translate a form of entertainment into learning experiences.
Express ideas, thoughts and emotions.

Each generation of young people is music oriented and develops its own favorite music "sound." In an effort to use music as a Bible Learning Activity, some of the music-related activities suggested in this chapter allow learners to change the music score so that it means more to them. Other activities invite the learners to look beyond the music score to the lyrics of a hymn or song for a learning experience. Some encourage the learners to make hymns more meaningful by changing the words.

Many of the suggested activities do not require musical talent or ability but simply a willingness to try something different. Recognize music as a learning medium. How it fulfills so many of the learners' basic and spiritual needs is indicated by the following chart.

Some learners have the creative talent to complete any of the following suggested activities by themselves; other learners do not. Therefore, use these ideas in small

A MUSIC BIBLE LEARNING ACTIVITY

PHYSICAL	SECURITY	SOCIAL	SELF-RESPECT	ACHIEVEMENT	SPIRITUAL
—allows learners to move around —provides a relaxed learning atmosphere	—helps develop a good mental attitude —provides a reachable goal —provides a learning experience	—allows for friendly exchange of ideas —provides fellowship —allows conversation —encourages helping one another —allows learners to work together	—allows expression of individual ideas —allows use of talents and skills —provides for giving and receiving recognition, understanding, respect, courtesy, appreciation, acceptance, and praise	—provides for using one's capabilities —encourages creativity —causes growth in knowledge	—integrates faith and expression —encourages the study of what others have felt about their faith —encourages use of God-given talent —helps learners understand the Psalms

groups. Five or six learners working together usually can complete such difficult assignments as writing an original song in thirty minutes or less! Teach conversationally by asking questions and offering suggestions where needed.

Follow each of these activities with a group discussion to reinforce the learning which has taken place during the assignment. Plan for diads, small or large group discussions.

HYMN PARAPHRASE (A,B,C;7-12;S-L)

A paraphrase is a rewording of thoughts, ideas or feelings already expressed in writing. As the title suggests, learners paraphrase hymns in this activity.

DISCOVERING HYMN PARAPHRASES

Working in small groups, learners read and discuss a hymn and decide what main ideas the songwriter was trying to convey. Then the hymn is paraphrased into words which better communicate the songwriter's ideas to today's youth.

Each small group shares and discusses their paraphrases with the others.

EXPLORING HYMN PARAPHRASE POSSIBILITIES

Based on the session goals and the specific needs of the learners, hymn paraphrases can:
1. Introduce, explore and illustrate the main points of the session or unit.
2. Indicate the levels of the learners' understanding concerning the session topic.
3. Personalize and encourage the application of the session truths.

CHECKLIST OF MATERIALS NEEDED

_____ Lined paper
_____ Pencils
_____ Hymnbook, songbook or sheet music
_____ Clear instructions

LYRIC RESPONSE (A,B,C;7-12;S-L)

Learners listen to or study a song, then respond to the lyrics.

DISCOVERING LYRIC RESPONSE

Learners listen to a hymn that poses a question (e.g., "Have You Any Room for Jesus?" or "Is Your All on the Altar?") and work in small groups composing an honest response to the lyrics.

EXPLORING LYRIC RESPONSE POSSIBILITIES

Based on the session aims and the specific needs of the learners, this activity can be planned to:
1. Introduce, explore, illustrate or summarize the central truths of the session Scriptures.
2. Encourage learners to make a personal commitment for Christ.

CHECKLIST OF MATERIALS NEEDED

_____ Lined paper
_____ Pencils
_____ Hymnbooks, songbooks, or sheet music
_____ Clear instructions
and sometimes . . .
_____ Recording
_____ Player for the recording

LYRIC WRITING (B,C;10-12;S-L)

Learners work in small groups writing words for a hymn expressing the central truths of the session, which fit a familiar tune.

DISCOVERING LYRIC WRITING

Allow learners to use any tune they wish, even if it is not in the hymnbook. But expect them to take the activity seriously.

The famous Charles Wesley, a hymn writer with over six thousand songs to his credit, frequently used this technique when writing lyrics for a new hymn.

Lyrics are shared and discussed.

EXPLORING LYRIC WRITING POSSIBILITIES

Based on the session goals and the specific needs of the learners, lyric writing can help learners:

1. Express their personal faith and share it with others.
2. Wrestle with and comprehend the central truth of the session or unit.
3. Explore or summarize the session Scriptures.

CHECKLIST OF MATERIALS NEEDED

_____ Lined paper
_____ Pencils
_____ Hymnbooks or other music
_____ Clear instructions

MUSICAL COMMERCIAL (A,C;9-12;S-L)

Small groups of learners compose a musical commercial, using a familiar commercial tune or making up an original tune. Assign topics for the commercials which relate to the session.

DISCOVERING MUSICAL COMMERCIALS

This Bible Learning Activity provides insight into what the learners value. Commercial writers assume that the products they advertise should be at the top of the consumers' priority lists. Note how much and what kind of conviction about their assigned "product" the learners show.

Commercials are shared and discussed with the other learners.

EXPLORING MUSICAL COMMERCIAL POSSIBILITIES

Based on the session goals and the specific needs of the learners, musical commercials can be planned to:

1. Familiarize learners with the session or unit or topic.
2. Illustrate or summarize the main point of the session study.
3. Define the spiritual values of the learners.

CHECKLIST OF MATERIALS NEEDED

_____ Lined paper
_____ Pencils
_____ Clear instructions

PSALM AND SONG MATCH (A,B;7-12;S-L)

Learners match up psalms and songs which have corresponding or contrasting messages.

DISCOVERING PSALM AND SONG MATCHES

Give each small group of learners a different psalm and tell them to find two or three corresponding hymns, songs, or choruses.

Each group then shares and discusses their choices with the other groups.

Psalm 150 and "Praise Him, Praise Him" by Fanny Crosby, illustrate this activity.

EXPLORING PSALM AND SONG POSSIBILITIES

Based on the session goals and the specific needs of the learners, this activity can:

1. Introduce, explore or illustrate the central truths of the session or unit.
2. Acquaint learners with the "hidden blessings" in the book of Psalms.
3. Involve learners with the session Scriptures.

CHECKLIST OF MATERIALS NEEDED

_____ Lined paper
_____ Pencils
_____ Hymnbooks or other music
_____ Clear instructions

SCORE-LYRIC COMPARISON (A,9-12;L or S)

Learners listen to a recorded song and discuss whether the score expresses the same thought as the lyrics or if the music seems to detract from the words.

DISCOVERING SCORE-LYRIC COMPARISONS

If the learners feel that the music complements the lyrics, the discussion centers on the basic truths presented by the song and the ramifications and implications of those truths.

For example, the music and words of the chorus, "I'm So Happy and Here's the Reason Why" are well suited to each other.

On the other hand, if the learners feel the music detracts from the meaning of the words (i.e., the music is slow or goes down on the scale when expressing a happy or "up" thought) the learners discuss ways to improve the song.

The "improved song" is shared and discussed with the other learners.

EXPLORING SCORE-LYRIC COMPARISON POSSIBILITIES

Based on the session goals and the specific needs of the learners, this type of activity can help learners to:
1. Become familiar with the session Scriptures.
2. Examine closely the meanings of songs or hymns.
3. Learn the biblical basis for the song used.

CHECKLIST OF MATERIALS NEEDED

_____ Hymnbook or other music
_____ Clear instructions

SONG COMPARISON (B,C;7-12;L or S)

Learners compare songs related to the session topic.

DISCOVERING SONG COMPARISONS

Learners discuss and compare different songs written on the same topic by different writers from different time periods. This activity is suitable for either large or small groups.

For instance, in a unit on "New Life in Christ" songs about the Christian life are compared with each other and with the Scriptures. Learners contribute relevant stories from their own personal experiences to the discussion.

EXPLORING SONG COMPARISON POSSIBILITIES

Based on the session goals and the specific needs of the learners, song comparisons can be designed to:
1. Explore, or summarize the main points presented in the session Scriptures.
2. Familiarize learners with different ways of stating basic truths as expressed by several songwriters.

CHECKLIST OF MATERIALS NEEDED

_____ Hymnbooks or other music
_____ Clear instructions

SONGWRITING (B,C;10-12;S-L)

Small groups of learners write an original song (lyrics and tune) on an assigned topic.

DISCOVERING SONGWRITING

The learners start with a study of the topic:
1. What do the Scriptures say about it?
2. What is important about the topic?
3. What does it mean to the learners personally?

Then the groups write a song about the significance of the assigned topic. The quality of songs written by the learners as a result of Scripture study is usually surprisingly good!

Songs are shared and discussed with other learners.

EXPLORING SONGWRITING POSSIBILITIES

Based on the session goals and the specific needs of the learners, songwriting can help learners to:
1. Express and share their personal faith.
2. Explore, illustrate or summarize the central truths of the session or unit Scriptures.

CHECKLIST OF MATERIALS NEEDED

_____ Lined paper
_____ Pencils
_____ Music graph paper
_____ Clear instructions

TUNE-TEXT MIX (C;7-12;S-L)

Learners find and coordinate Scriptures and songs around a central theme.

DISCOVERING TUNE-TEXT MIXES

Assign each small group of learners a topic. Each group then selects hymns or songs and Scripture texts which illustrate the assigned topic and arrange them into an effective fifteen- to thirty-minute presentation. A recorder in each group writes up an outline of the suggested presentation and shares it with the other learners.

EXPLORING TUNE-TEXT MIX POSSIBILITIES

Based on the session goals and the specific needs of the learners, this type activity could be planned to:
1. Explore, illustrate, or summarize the session Scriptures.

CHECKLIST OF MATERIALS NEEDED

____ Lined paper
____ Pencils
____ Hymnbooks or other music
____ Clear instructions

TUNE WRITING (B,C;10-12;S-L)

Learners are asked to compose tunes for existing lyrics.

DISCOVERING TUNE WRITING

Assign each small group of learners a Scripture passage which records the words to a song sung by a Bible character. Each group writes an appropriate tune for the song or for a part of the song, and shares it with the others.

Tune writing is easier, sometimes, if the learners read and choose from several different versions of Scripture.

A few of the recorded Bible songs include:

Moses'—Deuteronomy 32;
Deborah and Barak's—Judges 5;
Hannah's—1 Samuel 2:1-10;

The Angels'—Luke 2:13,14;
Mary's—Luke 1:46-55; and
The song of the redeemed—Revelation 5:9,10; 19:1-7

EXPLORING TUNE WRITING POSSIBILITIES

Based on the session goals and the specific needs of the learners, tune writing can be designed to:
Explore, illustrate or express the session Scripture or truths.

CHECKLIST OF MATERIALS NEEDED

____ Music graph paper
____ Pencils
____ Clear instructions

MUSIC-RELATED ACTIVITIES ARE SUCCESSFUL WHEN TEACHERS:

1. Assemble needed materials before class, always bringing enough for a few extra learners.
2. Set up the room before class.
3. Allow enough time for the activity.
4. Write down several ideas of their own in case they need to help learners get started thinking.
5. Have an open mind about the learners' compositions.
6. Encourage and compliment learners whenever possible.
7. Show interest and enthusiasm.
8. Do not require individual learners to complete an assignment they feel is beyond their ability (e.g., writing an original song).
9. Do not make the activity so much work that the learners fail to enjoy it or to learn from it.
10. Do not force their own tastes and ideas on the learners.
11. Do not fail to tie in the activity with the lesson.

YOUR NOTES: (Complete this sentence.)

When I used music-related activities . . .

CHAPTER NINE

DISCOVER IT!

Research activities involve learners in reading and studying various resources to discover an answer or to complete an assignment.

USE RESEARCH BIBLE LEARNING ACTIVITIES TO:

Study a topic in depth.
Provide an opportunity for learners to learn for themselves by discovery.
Involve each learner in the Scriptures.

Sessions can be made more personally profitable if the learners get involved in a research assignment before session time. They can read the viewpoints of one or more assigned authors on the topic and can form an opinion of their own based on their research findings. In any event, through research, learners do contribute more actively to the session.

Learners retain knowledge they discover for themselves, write down and share with others.

Research assignments give the opportunity to assign exploration and decision questions which will develop biblical thinking and reasoning habits in the learners. This helps guide their progress in finding and applying spiritual truths. They will discover the answer to many basic questions about life in general which they are or will soon be facing. Under the prayerful direction of a teacher, learners can be helped to answer them in the light of God's truths.

Learners can find what a Christian author has written on the subject, can find what God's Word says on the subject and also write their own answers.

Research activities can serve the teacher well when he is planning how to meet basic and spiritual needs of his learners. The following chart shows some of the benefits of research activities.

Research assignments are limited only by the imagination of the teacher. Research can be an individual or small group assignment and can be done in or out of class. How it is handled depends upon the amount of work involved and the time needed to complete the assignment. Research is usually summarized in a written report and presented to the other learners as a springboard for discussion. Decide which type of discussion activity to use after each research activity. Should learners give their reports as a panel, a symposium, or in small groups? How can the other learners benefit the most from the research of one or two of the learners?

Research assignments completed out of class require a high degree of motivation for the learners. Here are some ways to motivate learners:

1. Start the research in class and extend its completion to "outside" time. There is usually more motivation to finish an incomplete assignment than to get around to doing a "homework assignment" from start to finish.

2. Plan the assignment so the learner can meet during the week with the other class members who are doing it. Ask learners to finish a part of the assignment on their own before the meeting with you to help coordinate the research.

3. Agree to do part of the research and to bring it to the midweek service, if the class members do the same.

4. Make any outside assignments "Bible-oriented" so learners will experience the thrill of discovering that the Bible is relevant to their own lives in today's world.

5. Make the goal of the research very obvious and important to the learners. If they are going to invest time and energy into the research, they must see how it can and will benefit them.

A RESEARCH BIBLE LEARNING ACTIVITY

PHYSICAL	SECURITY	SOCIAL	SELF-RESPECT	ACHIEVEMENT	SPIRITUAL
—allows learners to move around	—develops a good mental attitude —provides a learning experience —provides a reachable goal	—allows learners to work together —provides an opportunity to meet new people —allows conversation —allows learners to work alone sometimes —provides a chance to help each other	—helps learners become knowledgeable about a subject —allows learners to use their skills and talents —develops thinking and reasoning abilities —provides an opportunity for giving and receiving recognition, attention, respect, courtesy, appreciation, acceptance, and praise	—provides for fulfilling one's capabilities —develops potential —exposes learners to new ideas and theories	—allows learners to discover God's truths —provides for applying spiritual truths to practicalities —reinforces truths taught in class —strengthens faith as learning increases —creates an opportunity for more in-depth lessons —provides a way for "during-the-week" involvement with God's truths —provides a reason for talking to strangers about God's truths

6. Assign individual assignments as the result of questions the individual learners ask—especially when the learner's motivation seems already to be high, as in the case of a disagreement in class or with parents, or with you, the teacher!

BIBLE STUDY PROJECTS (B;11-12;S-L)

When the session truths have their basis in several passages of Scripture and learners need to be familiar with them all, a Bible study project is assigned. As the word project implies, this activity entails more than just a few minutes of research.

DISCOVERING BIBLE STUDY PROJECTS

Give small groups of learners a time limit to find out as much as they can about a specific topic in the Bible. In some cases, provide a list of Scripture references. Learners then share their findings in a large group discussion.

EXPLORING BIBLE STUDY PROJECT POSSIBILITIES

Based on the session goals and the specific needs of the learners, projects can:
1. Explore, develop, clarify and support the central truths of the session or unit.
2. Involve learners in discovering God's Word.

CHECKLIST OF MATERIALS NEEDED

_____ Duplicated copies of the assignment
_____ Lined paper
_____ Pencils
_____ Bible study tools (Bibles in various paraphrases or versions, concordances, atlases, Bible dictionaries and encyclopedias, commentaries)

CASE STUDY (A,B,C;7-12;S-L)

A case study is a hypothetical, but real-life problem, which is used as a learning tool.

DISCOVERING CASE STUDIES

Give small groups of learners a copy of a case study to analyze and write scriptural recommendations for the characters in the case study.

Each small group shares and discusses their suggestions with the others.

EXPLORING CASE STUDY POSSIBILITIES

Based on the session goals and the specific needs of the learners, case studies can help learners:

1. Become familiar with, discover, explore, demonstrate or summarize the central truths of the session or unit.
2. Apply scriptural answers to real-life problems.
3. Become involved in God's Word.

CHECKLIST OF MATERIALS NEEDED

_____ Duplicated copies of case study
_____ Lined paper
_____ Pencils
_____ Clear instructions

CENSUS (A,B,C;10-12;L or S)

Learners take a census of the neighborhood around the church to ascertain who their neighbors are and what they do. A census differs from a survey because it gathers facts; a survey ascertains opinions.

DISCOVERING CENSUS

The learners design the forms, take the census and compile the results under your supervision. Planning a census involves deciding what to ascertain about the community—in other words, the reason for the census, and creating the right questions.

For example, learners can take a census to locate all the eleventh and twelfth graders in the area and to find out which hobbies and sports interest them most.

An outreach program to reach these young people can then be planned around those activities and publicized in the neighborhood.

EXPLORING CENSUS POSSIBILITIES

Based on the session goals and the specific needs of the learners, this assignment could help learners:

1. Explore and understand the people in the neighborhood around the church.
2. Take responsibility for reaching out to others with God's truths.
3. Share their faith with others.

CHECKLIST OF MATERIALS NEEDED

_____ Duplicated copies of the census form
_____ Copies of instructions for completing the forms (for learners only)
_____ Pencils

EXPANDING PANEL (B,C;10-12;L-S)

This activity is a variation of the regular panel activity discussed in Chapter 4, involving greater research and a different style of presentation.

DISCOVERING EXPANDING PANELS

Choose a topic and assign four or five learners to serve as panel members, one or two weeks ahead of time. Each panel member researches one aspect of the topic and prepares a three to five-minute presentation for the session.

At the beginning of the next session the panel members sit at the front of the classroom facing the other learners, and present their reports.

After their reports they move back into small groups with the other learners. Generate discussion by asking for comments and questions from the other learners.

The discussion after the reports from the panel members can be done in small groups if at least one panel member is included in each small group.

EXPLORING EXPANDING PANEL POSSIBILITIES

Based on the session aims and the specific needs of the learners, expanding panels can be planned to:

1. Introduce, explore or clarify the main points of the lesson or unit.
2. Involve learners in God's Word.

CHECKLIST OF MATERIALS NEEDED

_____ Copies of a three- to five-part, out-of-class assignment

_____ **Reference list of resources for panel members to use for their research**

FIELD TRIP (A,B,C;7-12;L or S)

A field trip is an off-site learning experience designed to enhance the current unit of study. The trip can be during the session time or during the week.

DISCOVERING FIELD TRIPS

Help the learners select and plan a field trip which relates to the current unit of study. Such trips might involve visiting another church, an ancient history museum, attending a special youth rally, or even visiting and helping a home missionary on location.

If only one small group of learners go on the field trip they report what they learned to the other learners at the beginning of the next session.

EXPLORING FIELD TRIP POSSIBILITIES

Based on the session aims and the specific needs of the learners, field trips can help the class:
1. Understand the session truths better.
2. Practice helping others and giving of themselves.
3. Fellowship with other Christian young people.
4. Benefit from a dynamic speaker or an effective presentation in another church or at a rally.

CHECKLIST OF MATERIALS NEEDED

_____ Duplicated copies of field trip information (where the class is going, how to get there, what to bring, what to look for during the trip, the purpose of the field trip, who is leading, when it ends, etc.).

INDUCTIVE STUDY (B,C;9-12;L-S)

Inductive study involves learners in studying the Bible in a methodical and practical way. It follows the basic format of:
1. What does Scripture say?
2. What does it mean?
3. What does it mean to me?

DISCOVERING INDUCTIVE STUDY

Give small groups of learners a copy of the assignment and several Bible study tools.

A recorder in each group shares the essence of the groups' findings with the other learners.

Inductive Bible study can also be an individual, out-of-class assignment. Then during the session each learner shares his personal findings and conclusions.

EXPLORING INDUCTIVE STUDY POSSIBILITIES

Based on the session goals and the specific needs of the learners, inductive study assignments can be designed to:
1. Explore, clarify, and summarize the session Scripture passage.
2. Develop a study pattern for learners to use in their own personal study of God's Word.
3. Help learners to understand God's Word.

CHECKLIST OF MATERIALS NEEDED

_____ Lined paper
_____ Pencils
_____ Duplicated copies of the assignment

QUESTION RESEARCH (B,C;7-12;S)

Learners work in small groups making up five to ten questions on the session Scripture passage. Each small group works on one segment of the passage. After a few minutes, the questions are exchanged between groups, then answered.

DISCOVERING QUESTION RESEARCH

Making up questions for another group of learners requires an understanding of what is being said in the Scripture passage and is an excellent learning experience. This activity can be an out-of-class assignment, but is more likely to be completed in class.

EXPLORING QUESTION RESEARCH POSSIBILITIES

Based on the session goals and the specific needs of the learners, question research can:
1. Introduce, explore, review, or summarize the session Scripture;
2. Help learners to look for and find important truths in a Scripture passage.

CHECKLIST OF MATERIALS NEEDED

_____ Lined paper
_____ Pencils
_____ Clear instructions

REACTION SHEETS (A,B,C;7-12;S)

Bible reaction sheets are pictures or sketches of a Bible scene or situation which are incomplete enough to be ambiguous.

DISCOVERING REACTION SHEETS

The learners react to the scene by writing what they feel happened or what is missing from or wrong with the scene. Then they research the situation in the Scriptures and verify their reactions.

EXPLORING REACTION SHEET POSSIBILITIES

Based on the session aims and the specific needs of the learners, reaction sheets can help learners to:
1. Apply biblical principles to real-life situations.
2. Review the unit theme, study or Scriptures.
3. Check their recall of a biblical scene or story.

1. What do you feel about this situation?
2. Why do you suppose the manager felt the sign was needed?
3. Write the Scripture reference which tells you how to feel in a situation such as this.

1. Fill in the comments you think are being made in the above situation.
2. What would you feel if you were the visitor?
3. Why are appearances important to some people?
4. Does God care about appearances?
5. Write the Scripture references where you found your answer to question #4.

1. Fill in the boy's reply.
2. What might have caused the father to be so angry?
3. Write 2-3 Scripture references which the boy should remember in this situation.
4. Write 2-3 Scripture references the father should remember in this situation.

CHECKLIST OF MATERIALS NEEDED

_____ Duplicated copies of two or three reaction sheets
_____ Pencils

**RESEARCH ACTIVITIES ARE SUCCESSFUL WHEN
TEACHERS:**

1. Assemble needed materials before the session.
2. Set up the room before the session.
3. Choose a worthwhile research assignment.
4. Write clear instructions.
5. Make sure learners understand the assignment.
6. Allow learners to choose their own assignments when making several different ones at the same time.

AND WHEN TEACHERS DO NOT:

1. Look for and reinforce only their own ideas.
2. Limit the creativity of their learners.
3. Forget to follow through and remind learners after making an assignment.
4. Be too helpful and end up doing the assignment themselves.
5. Arbitrarily plan field trips without consulting the learners.

YOUR NOTES: (Complete this sentence.)

When I used research activities . . .

CHAPTER TEN

ENJOY IT!

Creative testing and evaluating activities are techniques designed to measure the progress of the learners and the effectiveness of the teacher. They can also be helpful as Bible Learning Activities if planned appropriately.

USE CREATIVE TESTS OR EVALUATIVE ACTIVITIES TO:

Check the amount of knowledge a learner has acquired as a result of the class sessions.
Detect attitudinal changes resulting from classroom experiences with Bible Learning Activities.
Measure the skills developed by the learner.
Provide feedback from the learners which will help you improve your teaching.
Provide feedback to the learner about his learning.
Provide both learners and you with an enjoyable way to accomplish the above goals.

The session is not over for you when the final buzzer sounds and the last learner leaves the classroom. You have one more job to do—evaluate the session!
You can answer some of these questions if you were very observant during the session and if you listened carefully to what the learners said during the hour. But there are also some other accurate ways to test the amount of learning which occurred and to evaluate your effectiveness: Get input from the learners themselves. Use creative tests!!!

Creative tests are fun! They are challenging, but also rewarding, like a game! People love to play games which test their knowledge or skills. Creative tests allow learners to see how much progress they have made after one session or over a period of several sessions.

No teacher wants to waste valuable session time with ineffective teaching methods. Therefore, in order to be the best he can be and to help his learners grow both spiritually and as a person, a wise teacher uses creative testing and evaluation activities. Such activities fulfill the basic and spiritual needs of learners as outlined on the following chart.

A teacher should always prepare carefully for any Bible Learning Activity used during the session, but perhaps extra care should be taken when planning a testing activity.

BIBLE GAMES (A;7-12;S)

This activity uses the challenge of winning a game to enhance the learning of biblical truths and facts.

DISCOVERING BIBLE GAMES

Set up the classroom into several small circles with a table in the center of each. Set up a different Bible game on each table. As they enter, learners choose a game they wish to play and sit at the table.

Before class time, substitute clue cards for those provided with the game. Use memory verses and questions based on recent lessons as clues for playing the Bible games on review day.

The game rules remain the same, only the clue cards are changed.

EXPLORING BIBLE GAME POSSIBILITIES

Based on the session aims and the specific needs of the learners, Bible games can be planned to:
1. Introduce, explore or review the central truths or Scriptures of the unit or lesson.
2. Discover learning needs of class members in areas already covered by recent lessons.

A CREATIVE TESTING BIBLE LEARNING ACTIVITY

PHYSICAL	SECURITY	SOCIAL	SELF-RESPECT	ACHIEVEMENT	SPIRITUAL
—provides for a physical activity during the session	—provides a reachable goal for learners —helps sort out and organize ideas, facts and truths —allows use of knowledge, and skills —allows groups to form and work together	—allows fun and fellowship which make learning fun —allows meaningful and profitable conversation and discussion of ideas after writing —allows for friendly exchange of ideas	—promotes understanding and acceptance of self and others —invites recognition, attention, appreciation and praise —helps learners become aware of the lacks in their learning experience —develops thinking and reasoning abilities	—allows using one's capabilities —provides challenging opportunities and experiences —allows discovery of one's potential —sets the stage for gaining insight and new knowledge —encourages individual thought	—summarizes learning —underlines truths in learners' minds —allows teacher to check understanding of the learners —helps teacher and learners see amount of progress in acquiring knowledge, and skills

CHECKLIST OF MATERIALS NEEDED

_____ Two or more Bible games from the church library, with substituted questions or Bible verse cards based on the current unit of study.

_____ Clear instructions.

CHART REVIEW (A,B;7-12;L)

If a specific chart with several items of information has been used extensively during the unit of study, a chart review is an appropriate testing activity.

DISCOVERING CHART REVIEWS

Each key section of the chart is covered with a blank paper held in place with a small piece of masking tape.

Learners volunteer to tell what is behind each piece of blank paper or else call on classes of learners for their answers. As each answer is given, one of the pieces of blank paper is removed and the answer verified.

EXPLORING CHART REVIEW POSSIBILITIES

Based on the session aims and the specific needs of the learners, chart review can:

Remind learners of important facts and of the various factual relationships represented on the chart and covered in the various sessions.

CHECKLIST OF MATERIALS NEEDED

_____ A chart used during the unit or lesson

_____ Several strips of blank paper

_____ Masking tape

_____ Clear instructions

CHOOSE YOUR PROJECT (C;7-12;S-L)

Learners are given several options and allowed to choose which Bible Learning Activity they will participate in during the session.

DISCOVERING THE PROJECTS

Set up the classroom into four small circles with each circle marked with a large sign: Art, Drama, Writing and Research. As class members come into the classroom they go to the circle of their choice. Provide a resource table with supplies such as commentaries, maps, poster board, paints, felt pens, paper, pencils, etc.

The small groups work for thirty-five minutes preparing a project to share with the other learners which illustrates something about the unit. Give each group several suggestions to choose from to get the group started thinking and planning their presentation.

The presentations are made for the *Conclusion and Decision* phase of the session.

EXPLORING PROJECT POSSIBILITIES

Based on the session aims and the specific needs of the learners, projects can help learners:
1. Explore, review, or summarize the central truths of the lesson or unit.
2. Use their artistic, writing or dramatic talents.
3. Share with each other.

CHECKLIST OF MATERIALS NEEDED

Any supplies the learners will need to complete a writing, art, drama, or research project
Clear instructions

CLASS EVALUATION QUESTIONNAIRE (C;7-12;L or S)

Each learner provides feedback regarding the quarter by filling out a questionnaire. Collect the completed questionnaires and review them after the session.

DISCOVERING CLASS EVALUATION QUESTIONNAIRES
Stub-end questions are most effective.

EXPLORING CLASS EVALUATION POSSIBILITIES
Based on the unit goals and the specific needs of the learners, this type of questionnaire can be designed to:
1. Check the learning of the class members.

2. Determine the effectiveness of the teacher and help them in planning future lessons and Bible Learning Activities.

CHECKLIST OF MATERIALS NEEDED

_____ Copies of Class Evaluation Questionnaire
_____ Pencils
_____ Clear instructions

PROGRESSIVE QUIZ (A,B;7-10;L)

A progressive quiz administers test questions in an excitingly different way.

DISCOVERING PROGRESSIVE QUIZZES

Before the session, write ten questions on 3"x5" cards (one question to a card). Then tape the questions on various objects around the classroom.

Learners number from 1 to 10 on their papers, then move around the room finding and answering the test questions. Questions need not be answered in sequence because the answer to each question is written next to the corresponding number on the learner's paper.

If space is limited, a circular seating arrangement is used with the test questions taped to the chair backs. Learners move around the circle, exchanging seats to read and answer a new question.

Several types of questions to use for a progressive quiz are discussed in the Question suggestion in this chapter.

EXPLORING PROGRESSIVE QUIZ POSSIBILITIES

Based on the lesson or unit aims and the specific needs of the learners, this activity can:

1. Introduce, explore or review the main points of the unit or lesson.
2. Measure the amount of knowledge learners have assimilated about the unit topic.
3. Determine the effectiveness of the teacher's techniques.

CHECKLIST OF MATERIALS NEEDED

_____ Lined paper
_____ Pencils
_____ Ten 3"x5" cards with one test question on each
      card
_____ Masking tape
_____ Clear instructions

QUESTIONS (A,B,C;7-12;S,L,L-S or S-L)

There are numerous ways to use questions! In fact most of the Bible Learning Activities suggested in this book involve using questions. Questions can be answered verbally or in writing, by individual learners or by a small group of learners. If answered individually, questions are then discussed in small groups; if answered in small groups, they are discussed in a large group!

Tricky questions are a challenge to some learners, but a source of resentment to others. So tricky questions should be avoided when planning a quiz. The correct answer, however, should not be too obvious.

DISCOVERING QUESTIONS

Five basic types of questions are discussed below.

MULTIPLE CHOICE: Before taking a quiz, tell the learners whether or not there will be one or more than one correct choice for each question. When more than one choice is correct, learners need to evaluate carefully each question and choice; the quiz becomes an excellent learning experience.

Here are some samples based on Acts 1—12 (correct answers are marked with an asterisk):

1) Acts was
    *A. Written by Luke
    *B. Written about Luke and his friends
    C. Written while Luke was in jail
    *D. Written while Luke was alive
    E. Read to Luke by his grandmother
2) The Ascension
    A. Happened at Pentecost

    B. Happened after Pentecost
    C. Was caused by Pentecost
    *D. Happened ten days before Pentecost
    E. Is another name for Pentecost

FILL-IN-THE-BLANKS: Test learners on specific details with fill-in-the-blanks questions. Be sure that those details are worth memorizing by the learners.

TRUE-OR-FALSE: True-or-false questions used to test factual learning are difficult to write! Either the answer seems too obvious or the question is a little tricky!

Therefore, a better use for true-or-false questions is to generate a lively discussion with statements which are ambiguous enough to be either true or false based on the individual learner's interpretation of and assumptions about the question. True or false questions used this way are often called "Agree/Disagree" (see **Agree/Disagree, Chapter 4 "Discuss It!"**).

ESSAY: Carefully used, essay questions can be effective, especially with older youth. The learner is required to give some thought to his answer, but is not expected to write more than one or two short paragraphs per question. No more than one or two essay questions are assigned to each learner. Each learner can be given different questions, however.

STUB-END: Attitudes and opinions are often difficult to check! Help the learners express and compare their opinions by providing several stub-end questions to be answered and then discussed.

Stub-end questions help the learners with self-evaluation and give them insight into themselves.

The following stub-end questionnaire can be used as an approach activity to a unit of study on the Bible as God's Word. By changing the wording slightly it could be used at the beginning and end of a unit or any individual book of the Bible. (If the same questionnaire is given at the end of the unit, the learners can note attitudinal or habit changes in their lives.)

    1. My favorite part of the Bible is _____
    2. I wish the Bible could _____
    3. I read the Bible whenever _____
    4. Reading the Bible is _____
    5. The hardest part of the Bible to understand is _____

EXPLORING QUESTION POSSIBILITIES

Based on the lesson goals and the specific needs of the learners, questions can be designed to:

1. Introduce, explore, illustrate, summarize, or review the main points or Scriptures of the unit or lesson.
2. Measure the knowledge level of the learners on specific topics.
3. Determine a teacher's effectiveness.
4. Measure attitudinal or life changes of the learners after a series of lessons.

CHECKLIST OF MATERIALS NEEDED

_____ Selected well-planned test questions
_____ Lined paper or duplicated test or questions
_____ Pencils
_____ Clear instructions
and sometimes . . .
_____ Specific materials required for a special activity involving questions

SCRAMBLED VERSES (A,C;7-12;L or S)

Learners are tested on their memory verses with a scrambled verse activity.

DISCOVERING SCRAMBLED VERSES

One way to use scrambled Bible memory verses is to duplicate copies of the scrambled verses and to let the learners work individually or in small groups to unscramble them and locate the Scripture references for each verse.

A more active use of scrambled Bible memory verses uses two or more teams competing against each other for speed and accuracy. Write each Bible memory verse on 3"x5" cards (one word to a card) and place all the cards for one verse in an envelope. Make identical sets of scrambled Bible memory verses for each team. Give each small group the first envelope of their set and say "Go!" Learners open the envelopes and work together arranging the cards in the proper order. The first team to unscramble the verse wins a point and reads the verse aloud.

Then the teacher gives each small group their second envelope and the game (or test!) continues.

EXPLORING SCRAMBLED VERSE POSSIBILITIES

Based on the unit goals and the specific needs of the learners, scrambled verses can help learners:
1. Review their memory verses.
2. Check how well they have memorized the assigned verses.

CHECKLIST OF MATERIALS NEEDED

_____ Duplicated copies of scrambled verses
_____ Pencils
_____ Clear instructions

Or sometimes . . .

_____ Two or three sets of scrambled verses written on 3"x5" cards (one word to a card)
_____ Several envelopes

CREATIVE TESTING AND EVALUATION ACTIVITIES ARE SUCCESSFUL WHEN TEACHERS:

1. Assemble the needed supplies before the session.
2. Set up the classroom before the session.
3. Prepare carefully.
4. Show enthusiasm.
5. Encourage learners to use the test to see what they have learned.
6. Allow the test activity to be as informal as possible and still be effective.
7. Use test results to evaluate their own teaching as well as the learners' growth.

AND WHEN TEACHERS DO NOT:

1. Make a test too difficult and unpleasant.
2. Test only for rote memory answers.
3. Forget that even a test can be a learning activity.
4. Give tests just because someone says they must— the teacher must believe in tests himself before they will be effective.

YOUR NOTES: (COMPLETE THIS SENTENCE.)

When I used Creative Testing activities . . .